HEIDELBERG

Travel Guide
2023

Marcus A. Morgan

Your Passport to Memorable Adventures: Unlocking the Beauty of the City's Delights and Unveiling the Hidden Gems of Heidelberg

TABLE OF CONTENTS

1. INTRODUCTION

Heidelberg is a delightful city that enchants visitors with its rich history, beautiful architecture, and romantic atmosphere. It is located in the gorgeous Neckar River Valley. Heidelberg, which is well-known for its picturesque surroundings and offers a perfect fusion of old-world charm and modern refinement, is a must-visit location for tourists looking for a special experience.

The Heidelberg University, one of Europe's oldest and most prominent universities, has a history spanning more than 800 years and is located in Heidelberg.

This prestigious school has drawn academics, thinkers, and learners from all over the world, adding to the city's thriving intellectual and cultural atmosphere.

The Heidelberg Castle, which is majestically placed on a hill above the city, is one of Heidelberg's most recognizable attractions. This majestic castle complex offers amazing views of the surrounding countryside and boasts a lengthy history. Visitors can immerse themselves in the histories of the monarchs, conquerors, and intellectuals who once roamed its halls by exploring the ruins.

The Old Town (Altstadt) of the city is home to a wealth of historical landmarks, winding cobblestone lanes, and quaint squares. It is delightful to stroll through its lanes, admire the immaculate preservation of the buildings, and find secret courtyards and charming nooks. Heidelberg's skyline landmark, the Church of the Holy Spirit, serves as a reminder of the area's rich religious and architectural history.

The appeal of Heidelberg goes beyond its historical sites. With picturesque parks, gardens, and the alluring Neckar River, the city is also well known for its breathtaking natural beauty. The Philosophers' Walk, a calm riverfront promenade with panoramic city views, is a well-liked location for reflection and relaxation.

Festivals and cultural events make Heidelberg's calendar lively all year long. There is always something to fascinate the senses and connect with the city's cultural fabric, from music festivals to art exhibitions and theatrical performances.

Heidelberg offers a wide variety of traditional German cuisine and regional delicacies, making it a haven for foodies. The food scene in Heidelberg is sure to please any pallet, with everything from robust sausages and pretzels to delicious pastries and regional wines.

Heidelberg guarantees a genuinely remarkable experience, whether you choose to explore its historical landmarks, indulge in its delectable cuisine, or simply stroll through its picturesque streets. Visitors are enchanted by the mood it produces, which has an enduring impact because of its distinctive fusion of history, culture, and natural beauty. So, come and see Heidelberg's magnificence as you set off on a journey packed with cherished experiences and fascinating discoveries.

1.1 Learning about Heidelberg's Attraction and Charm

Travelers are drawn to Heidelberg, a treasure located in the middle of Germany, by its attractiveness and beauty.

This charming city offers a plethora of activities that enthrall visitors from all over the world. It is the ideal fusion of history, culture, and natural beauty.

Heidelberg's magnificent architecture is one of its most alluring features. The Old Town (Altstadt) is a remarkable example of the city's well-preserved architecture.

Visitors are taken back in time as they stroll through the city's winding cobblestone streets, which are lined with exquisitely decorated buildings, elaborate fountains, and quaint squares. A piece of history is revealed at each step, inspiring awe and amazement.

The Heidelberg Castle is without a doubt the jewel in the crown of Heidelberg's architectural splendor. This beautiful fortification, perched atop a hill, attracts attention with its majesty and spectacular views of the city.

The Gothic and Renaissance buildings on the castle grounds, which relate stories of medieval knights, royal residences, and educational pursuits, provide an insight into the city's colorful past.

The natural beauty of Heidelberg is equally alluring. The city's meandering Neckar River adds a sense of peace and calm. A boat ride or leisurely stroll along its banks will provide you with stunning views of the city's skyline and beautiful surroundings.

Poets, philosophers, and thinkers throughout history have drawn inspiration from the panoramic views that can be seen from The Philosophers' Walk, a picturesque route tucked away on the other side of the river.

The city's rich cultural tapestry only heightens its appeal. Thanks to its esteemed university, which has created a thriving academic and creative community, Heidelberg is known as a center of study and intellectual pursuits.

Visitors have the opportunity to fully immerse themselves in the city's rich cultural legacy thanks to the abundance of art galleries, museums, and theaters. There is always something to excite the intellect and arouse the senses, from classical performances to contemporary art displays.

The inviting atmosphere of Heidelberg adds to its appeal. Visitors are welcomed with open arms by the community, which is renowned for its friendliness and hospitality, and are made to feel like members of the Heidelberg family.

The city's thriving social scene, busy cafes, and bustling markets foster an appealing environment that promotes discovery and interaction.

Heidelberg has a charm that stays with you, whether you're exploring the ancient alleys, marveling at the majestic castle, or simply taking in the beauty of nature.

It is a place that truly captures the hearts of those who are fortunate enough to encounter it because of its ageless beauty and enchanting charm. So come and experience Heidelberg's charm and attraction, where history, culture, and natural beauty converge to create an experience that will never be forgotten.

1.2 Travelers' Practical Information

To ensure a hassle-free and enjoyable trip to Heidelberg, it is imperative to arm yourself with useful knowledge before setting off on your journey. ***Keep in mind the following important information:***

- **Visa Requirements:** Before flying to Germany, find out if you need a visa for your home country. Make sure your passport is valid for at least six months past the duration of your intended stay and check if you need a visa.

- **Accessibility:** Heidelberg is easily reached by a variety of modes of transportation. Frankfurt Airport (FRA), which is about 90 kilometers distant and the closest significant airport if traveling by air, is the closest one. From there, you can take a train, bus, or vehicle to get to Heidelberg. It is easy to move around the city thanks to the effective public transit system, which includes trams and buses.

- **Weather Considerations:** When making travel plans to Heidelberg, consider the local weather. The city has a moderate climate, with chilly winters and mild to warm summers. In accordance with the time of year you will be visiting, pack a variety of clothing, including both light and warm items.
Always check the weather prediction as you get closer to your travel dates.

- **Currency and Money Issues:** The Euro (€) is the country of Germany's official currency. Make sure you have enough cash on hand or that you can access ATMs to withdraw money. Although most businesses accept credit and debit cards, it's still a good idea to have some cash on hand for smaller shops or vendors that might not.

- **Language:** German is Heidelberg's official tongue. Even though most people understand English, it's helpful to learn a few fundamental German greetings and phrases.

Your relationships with locals can be improved and your trip will be more enjoyable as a result.

- **Security and Safety:** Travelers generally feel safe in Heidelberg. However, it is always advisable to follow standard safety precautions, such as being alert of your surroundings, keeping a check on your valuables, and choosing secure transit choices. Learn the local emergency phone numbers so you'll know who to call in case of any emergencies.

- **Health and Medical Facilities:** Before visiting Heidelberg, it's a good idea to get travel insurance that includes medical coverage. As recommended by your nation, make sure you have the required vaccines. In case you have any health issues while you're there, be familiar with the locations of the local hospitals and clinics.

- **Electrical Outlets:** Germany uses 230V at a frequency of 50Hz as its standard voltage. The power outlets are Type C and Type F, and they take Schuko and Euro plugs. If any of your electronic equipment uses a different plug type, think about packing a universal adaptor.

- **Central European Time (CET):** which is UTC+1 during standard time and UTC+2 during daylight saving time, is the time zone in which Heidelberg is located. When you get here, set your clocks properly.

You may make sure that your vacation to Heidelberg is joyful and hassle-free by taking into account these practical factors before leaving.

In order to build lasting memories in this engaging location, remember to organize your itinerary, make the required reservations, and experience the city's many attractions, cultural landmarks, and gastronomic pleasures.

2. LANDMARKS OF HEIDELBERG TO EXPLORE

The historically significant city of Heidelberg is home to an incredible array of attractions that highlight its rich cultural past. Each monument, from imposing castles to charming streets, offers a different perspective on the city's past. ***Here are some of Heidelberg's must-see attractions:***

1. Heidelberg Castle: Perched on a hilltop above the city, Heidelberg Castle is a recognizable representation of the magnificence of the place. This spectacular ruin displays Gothic and Renaissance architectural styles. Visit the Great Barrel, one of the largest wine barrels in the world, explore the castle's courtyards, and take in the breathtaking views of Heidelberg from the castle terrace.

2. Heidelberg's Old Town (Altstadt): is the city's historic core and is a picturesque tangle of cobblestone streets, well-preserved structures, and bustling squares.

Take a stroll through Europe's longest pedestrian street, the Hauptstrasse, which is surrounded by stores, cafes, and restaurants. Visit the Church of the Holy Spirit, a stunning example of late Gothic architecture, or explore the Market Square (Marktplatz), which features a spectacular town hall in the Renaissance style.

3. The Philosopher's Walk: From this picturesque walkway on the other side of the Neckar River, you can see Heidelberg in all its glory. The Philosopher's Walk got its moniker because it was a favored place for Heidelberg's intellectuals to stroll leisurely while reflecting on the important issues in life. Take a leisurely stroll along the route that is bordered with trees while taking in the expansive views of the city and its surroundings.

4. Karl Theodor Bridge (Old Bridge): The Karl Theodor Bridge spans the Neckar River and connects the Old Town to the Neuenheim neighborhood. Beautiful views of the river, the castle, and the metropolis may be had from this pedestrian bridge.

Cross the bridge at your leisure and take in the lovely ambiance that has influenced countless writers and artists.

5. Student   Jail   (Studentenkarzer): Formerly a place of punishment for rowdy students, the Student Jail is now an intriguing museum. This unusual monument, which is close to Heidelberg University, provides a window into students' lives in the past. Admire the graffiti and inscriptions that have survived on the cell walls, which offer an insight into the old-school student scene.

6. Jesuit   Church   (Jesuitenkirche): Heidelberg is home to this wonderful baroque church, which is a hidden gem. Beautiful frescoes, delicate stucco work, and magnificent altars decorate the interior. As you tour this architectural wonder, be in awe of the skill and serene atmosphere.

These famous sites only serve as a small sample of Heidelberg's extensive cultural legacy; this guide will go into greater detail about some of the above-mentioned sites.

Numerous additional historical landmarks, architectural marvels, and undiscovered jewels will be revealed as you explore the city, adding to its attraction.

The landmarks of Heidelberg will transport you to a bygone period as you immerse yourself in the history, take in the breathtaking views, and make lifelong memories.

2.1 Heidelberg Castle: Majestic Fortress with Panoramic Views

Heidelberg Castle stands as a spectacular tribute to the magnificence and history of Heidelberg, perched high on a hill above the city.

One of Germany's most well-known sites, this renowned castle complex draws tourists from all over the world to marvel at its architectural splendor and expansive vistas of the city and Neckar River.

The castle was built as a fortification to defend the city in the 13th century, which is when it first appeared. Under the Electors of the Palatinate's sponsorship, it developed through the years into a beautiful Renaissance palace.

The War of the Palatinate Succession in the late 17th century did, however, do significant damage to the castle, which was further destroyed by lightning strikes and successive fires. The castle's current state as an outstanding ruin only serves to enhance its attractiveness and charm.

It seems like traveling back in time to explore Heidelberg Castle. You will come across architectural wonders that represent several architectural eras, such as Gothic, Renaissance, and Baroque, as you stroll around its spacious courtyards.

The Otto Heinrich Building displays the Renaissance glory of the castle with its elaborate facade and lovely arcades. The Friedrich Building provides a look into the Baroque era with its magnificent staircase and ornate accents.

The Great Barrel, a massive wine barrel stored in the castle's cellar, is one of its most well-known attractions. One of the biggest wine barrels in the world, the "Heidelberg Tun," can carry more than 200,000 liters of wine. The barrel serves as a popular photo location for tourists and is a tribute to the long-standing wine-making heritage in the area.

The panoramic views from the castle, though, are what really stop you in your tracks. You may take in the expansive views of Heidelberg's roofs, the Neckar River, and the surrounding countryside from the castle terrace. When the sun sets, the scene is exceptionally beautiful since the city is bathed in a golden glow.

In addition to being a visual treat, Heidelberg Castle is also rich in historical and cultural value. The castle is home to the Heidelberg Castle Museum, which displays a sizable collection of artifacts, including weapons, works of art, and medieval relics, and offers unique insights into the history of the castle.

Visitors can become fully immersed in the historical tales of the castle and learn more about its significance to Heidelberg and the Palatinate region.

You have two options for getting to Heidelberg Castle: either take a leisurely stroll through the Old Town's meandering lanes or use the funicular railway, which offers a beautiful ascent.

Regardless of the route you take, the anticipation that grows with each step as you slowly ascend toward the castle makes the journey a memorable aspect of the experience.

Anyone exploring the city must pay a visit to Heidelberg Castle. It's an opportunity to take in stunning vistas, marvel at the beauty of Renaissance and medieval architecture, and learn more about Heidelberg's fascinating past.

Get ready to be amazed by Heidelberg Castle's grandeur as you learn about a genuine gem of German cultural history.

2.2 Old Town (Altstadt): Cobblestone Streets and Historical Sites Make Up

Spend some time in Heidelberg's Old Town (Altstadt), where the cobblestone streets, intact houses, and fascinating historical landmarks bring history to life. With its wealth of architectural treasures and historical sites, this lovely neighborhood is a delight for both history buffs and unhurried travelers.

You'll be taken back in time as soon as you approach the Old Town, surrounded by a tapestry of exquisitely decorated facades, bustling squares, and charming passageways.

The Old Town's bustling spine is the Hauptstrasse, one of the longest pedestrian streets in Europe. It is dotted with a variety of stores, boutiques, cafes, and restaurants.

Enjoy a leisurely stroll down this vibrant street while indulging in some retail therapy or sampling the regional cuisine.

The Rathaus, a Renaissance-style town hall, radiates from the Market Square (Marktplatz), which is the Old Town's central location. Take in the vibrant atmosphere of the square as you admire the fine features of this architectural marvel, especially on market days when vendors sell fresh fruit, flowers, and regional crafts.

The Church of the Holy Spirit (Heiliggeistkirche) is one of the Old Town's must-see attractions. This massive late Gothic church dominates the skyline and serves as a representation of Heidelberg thanks to its complex spire. Enter to behold the magnificent stained glass windows, elaborate woodwork, and serene atmosphere. You may get sweeping views of the Old Town and the surrounding area from the church's tower.

Another well-known sight in the Old Town is the Old Bridge (Alte Brücke), also referred to as the Karl Theodor Bridge. This pedestrian bridge, which spans the Neckar River, provides beautiful views of the city, the river, and the castle.

Take a leisurely stroll across the bridge, possibly pausing to see the statue of the monkey on the Heidelberg Bridge, which is thought to bring luck to anybody who touches it.

More hidden treasures can be found by exploring the Old Town's little side alleyways and secret passages. Discover magnificently preserved Renaissance structures with elaborate facades and detailed architectural elements, such as the Knight St. George House (Ritter St. Georg Haus) or the House of the Knights (Haus Zum Ritter).

Admire the decorative fountains that give the Old Town squares their charm and personality, such the Hercules Fountain and the Market Fountain.

Don't pass up the chance to check out the Student Jail (Studentenkarzer), a one-of-a-kind museum depicting Heidelberg University's disciplinary history. Unruly students used to be housed here, and their naughty inscriptions and graffiti are still visible on the cell walls, offering an intriguing look into student life in the past.

Beyond its architectural wonders, the Old Town captivates. It's a spot where you can enjoy the entertaining street performances, mingle with the people in outdoor cafes, and take in the energetic ambiance. Indulge in local specialities, such as the famous Heidelberg Student Kisses (Studentenküssen), a delectable chocolate treat, or enjoy a glass of regional wine at one of the quaint wine pubs.

The Old Town of Heidelberg is a fascinating fusion of culture, history, and vivacious energy. It is a location where the past and present collide, and around every turn, a tale just waiting to be unearthed.

So explore Heidelberg's Old Town as you stroll along its cobblestone streets, take in the area's rich history, and let the Old Town's attractiveness enchant you as you make lasting memories there.

2.3 The Church of the Holy Spirit: Ionic Symbol of Heidelberg.

The Church of the Holy Spirit (Heiliggeistkirche), which rises majestically in the center of Heidelberg's Old Town, serves as a recognizable representation of the city.

This magnificent late Gothic church serves as a place of worship as well as a reminder of Heidelberg's illustrious past and stunning architecture.

The Church of the Holy Spirit, with its imposing presence and ornate spire ascending towards the heavens, dominates the city's skyline. Its lengthy construction, which started in the 14th century and spanned many decades, produced a distinctive fusion of Gothic, Renaissance, and Baroque elements.

You will be mesmerized by the church's breathtaking magnificence as soon as you enter. A sense of grandeur and tranquility is produced by the tall vaulted ceilings, elaborate stained glass windows, and beautiful woodwork.
The interior of the church is adorned with an extensive collection of religious art, including altars, statues, and paintings that reflect the skill and commitment of the time's creators.

The Church of the Holy Spirit's famed pulpit, a masterpiece of Renaissance art, is one of its attractions. The pulpit is a main point of the church, catching people's eyes and attention with its intricate carvings of biblical subjects and artistic motifs.

The Church of the Holy Spirit's tower climb is rewarded with breath-taking panoramic views. The splendor of Heidelberg emerges in front of you as you ascend the twisting staircase.

You may admire the Old Town's gorgeous rooftops, the Neckar River's motion, and the city's surrounding hills from the viewing platform of the tower. It's a vantage point from which you may view Heidelberg's beauty from a different angle.

In addition to its stunning architecture, the Church of the Holy Spirit is significant in terms of culture and history. It has been there for major occasions throughout its history, such as the signing of the Heidelberg Catechism, a Protestant confessional document, in the late 16th century. This book continues to have an impact today and was crucial in forming the Reformed religion.

A unique opportunity to experience the spiritual and cultural atmosphere that permeates the building is to attend a service or concert at the Church of the Holy Spirit.

Regular services, organ recitals, and other musical events are held at the church, allowing guests to take in the serene ambiance and enjoy the acoustics of this holy place.

The Church of the Holy Spirit is more than just a house of worship; it also serves as a representation of Heidelberg's culture, history, and architectural legacy.

Visitors from all over the world come to view its magnificence, find comfort within its walls, and admire the craftsmanship of the past attracted by its eternal beauty and significance.

Visit the Church of the Holy Spirit when you are in Heidelberg if you enjoy history, architecture, or are just looking for some peace and quiet. Allow yourself to be moved by its enduring presence in the center of this magical city, as well as by its allure, spirituality, and charm.

3. UNVEILING HIDDEN GEMS

Beyond the well-known sites and well-liked attractions, Heidelberg is home to a wealth of undiscovered treasures. These less well-known attractions and activities give visitors a real and uncommon viewpoint on the city's hidden appeal.

The Philosophers' Walk (Philosophenweg), a picturesque path that snakes around the Heiligenberg hill's slopes and provides stunning views of the city and the Neckar River below, is one such undiscovered gem.

Philosophers and academics used to stroll along this peaceful walkway in search of inspiration, and today's visitors still find inspiration there.

Enjoy panoramic views while taking a leisurely stroll along the Philosophers' Walk, where you may lose yourself in nature.

The Kunstverein Heidelberg is a must-see for art lovers. This modern art gallery, hidden inside a historic structure, features cutting-edge and provocative creations by both regional and worldwide artists.

The gallery offers a venue for artistic expression and the pushing of creative boundaries by hosting recurring exhibitions, installations, and performances.

The German Pharmacy Museum, a hidden gem for history and science buffs, is also located in Heidelberg. This one-of-a-kind museum explores the history of pharmacy and is housed within Heidelberg Castle.

It features an amazing collection of antique pharmaceutical instruments, medical artifacts, and apothecary artifacts.

In this fascinating and instructive museum, learn about the development of medicine and gain insight into historical practices.

The lovely Neuenheim Market Square (Neuenheimer Marktplatz) is another undiscovered gem located in the Neuenheim neighborhood. This neighborhood hangout offers a calm ambiance and a lovely variety of cafes, boutiques, and speciality stores. Grab a coffee, peruse the boutiques, and take in the genuine neighborhood atmosphere.

Those who wander into the Student Prison (Studentenkarzer) will discover a secret culinary pleasure. This unusual museum, which is close to the university, showcases the academic background of Heidelberg's students.

Writings, artwork, and graffiti placed on the walls of the cells over the years by cheeky students decorate them. It provides a fascinating window into Heidelberg's vibrant history and customs of student life.

The Heiligenberg Hill offers a getaway into a serene haven outside of the city for nature lovers.

Discover ancient ruins, stroll through meandering forest pathways, and marvel at the remnants of the Heidenloch, a Celtic fortification. The hill offers a peaceful getaway that is ideal for hiking, having a picnic, or just taking in the scenery.

Indulge in the lively ambiance of the **Heidelberg Farmers' Market (Heidelberger Wochenmarkt),** which is the final recommendation. This thriving market comes to life with a variety of fresh vegetables, regional specialties, flowers, and handmade crafts and is situated in the shadow of the Church of the Holy Spirit.

Engage with the welcoming sellers, indulge in regional cuisine, and take in the vivacious atmosphere of this hidden gem.

Discovering Heidelberg's hidden treasures is like going on a treasure hunt, with each find bringing awe and excitement.

These undiscovered gems, which range from picturesque walks and secret overlooks to specialized museums and neighborhood markets, give you the chance to develop a closer relationship with the city and make priceless memories.

So take a detour, embrace your inner intrepid, and discover Heidelberg's secrets. Heidelberg is genuinely remarkable.

3.1   Heidelberg's Off-the-Beaten-Path Excursions

Heidelberg is well known for its majestic castle, quaint Old Town, and stunning river vistas, but the city also offers a variety of off-the-beaten-path excursions that provide adventurous visitors with an unforgettable and genuine experience.

Take a step back from the masses and explore Heidelberg's secret attractions.

- **Königstuhl:** One such excursion takes you to the Königstuhl, a peak in the city. Leaving the busy city streets behind, you may reach the peak for panoramic views over Heidelberg and the surrounding areas. Hike up the forest trails to the summit or take a picturesque trip on the Königstuhl Funicular. Explore the Königstuhl Observatory once you've arrived for a chance to learn about the wonders of astronomy and take in the night sky.

- **Erlenbusch Nature Park:** A trip to the Erlenbusch Nature Park is essential for nature lovers. This quiet park is a haven of lush woodlands, winding trails, and tranquil ponds and is situated outside of Heidelberg. Start a leisurely bike ride or stroll through the park, take in the beauty of the landscape, and keep an eye out for the variety of plants and animals that make this place home.

- **Heidelberg Thingstätte:** Visit the Heidelberg Thingstätte if you're looking for a historical adventure. Built during the Nazi era and used as a location for propaganda events, this open-air amphitheater is tucked away in the trees atop the Heiligenberg hill. It now serves as a distinctive and unsettling historical monument. Investigate the ruins, consider the history, and take in the amazing architecture of the amphitheater.

- **Neuenheim Cemetery:** Visit the Neuenheim Cemetery if you want to get a true sense of the neighborhood. This wonderfully designed burial place, in contrast to conventional cemeteries, is a tranquil sanctuary that honors the history and culture of the city. Explore the roads surrounded by magnificent tombstones, elaborate sculptures, and tranquil gardens. A quiet and contemplative setting, the cemetery offers a window into the lives and legacies of Heidelberg's citizens.

- **River Neckar**: Go kayaking or canoeing on the River Neckar for a sense of history and adventure intermingled. Paddle along serene waters, past beautiful scenery, and take in the city from a new angle. As you float across the river, you'll come across secret caverns and isolated nooks that provide a sense of peace amid the bustle of the city.

Finally, explore Heidelberg's secret murals and artistic expressions to delve into the city's thriving street art scene.

Explore the city's backstreets and alleyways while keeping an eye out for vibrant street art, breathtaking murals, and inspiring graffiti. Each artwork offers a different story and injects some imagination into the urban environment.

Heidelberg's off-the-beaten-path excursions let you explore beneath the surface and find the city's secret treasures.

These excursions provide you the ability to make memories that are one-of-a-kind and unforgettable, whether you choose to rise to breath-taking perspectives, immerse yourself in nature, visit historical sites, or embrace local art and culture.

So venture off the usual road, embrace your inner explorer, and let Heidelberg enchant and surprise you with its hidden gems.

3.2   Investigating Hidden Courtyards and Secret Alleyways

There is more to find as you explore Heidelberg's lovely streets than just the beaten roads. You are beckoned to set out on an adventure journey and solve the city's captivating mysteries through hidden courtyards and obscure pathways.

Enter the maze-like maze of alleys known as the **"Plöck"** and get ready to be whisked away to another time.

Historic structures, charming stores, and inviting cafés adorn this street's narrow, twisting lanes. Look for hidden courtyards tucked away behind inconspicuous doorways as you walk around its cobblestone pathways.

These quiet retreats from the busy city streets are frequently ornamented with lush vegetation, lovely buildings, and welcoming benches where you can sit and take in the atmosphere.

The Heuscheuer Building contains one of Heidelberg's most beautiful secret courtyards. Stepping into this serene area, known as the "Lutherhof," is like entering a completely different planet.

This architectural marvel is home to a hidden courtyard. The charming fountain, colorful flowers, and exquisite facades in the courtyard provide a tranquil setting that transports you back in time. Breathe in the still beauty that surrounds you and take a moment to examine the intricate intricacies of the nearby structures.

Within the Alte Universität (Old University), there is yet another undiscovered gem. A mysterious courtyard called the **"Hof des Alten Marstalls"** is hidden behind its opulent entryway. The rush and bustle of the metropolis is peacefully subdued by this hidden retreat.

The courtyard, which is enclosed by ivy-covered walls, radiates a sense of classic beauty. Relax on a bench among the statues and old buildings as you take in the peace and quiet of this hidden gem.

Keep an eye out for the **"Dreikönigsgasse,"** a secret alleyway that takes you on a trip through time with its restored medieval architecture and charming stores, as you explore the streets close to the Church of the Holy Spirit. Discover hidden courtyards along the cobblestone route, each with its own distinct personality and allure.

Enter the **"Platz der Spanier"** (Spanish Square)'s secret courtyard for a taste of the Mediterranean.

This charming area offers a Mediterranean feel replete with colorful facades, vine-covered walls, and pleasant outdoor seats hidden behind modest facades. Take in the lively atmosphere of this hidden hideaway while dining or sipping on a refreshing beverage at one of the attractive cafés.

Discovering Heidelberg's obscure courtyards and back alleys is like unearthing a hidden treasure trove of treats.

Whether it's a secret courtyard bursting with beauty or an enchanted passageway that piques your interest, every turn and turn unveils a new surprise. These undiscovered attractions provide visitors a sense of Heidelberg's fascinating past, stunning architecture, and the tranquil moments that may be found away from the busy streets.

So give yourself permission to stray from the usual road, enjoy the thrill of discovery, and let the city's secluded courtyards and shady lanes capture your imagination.

3.3 Calm Gardens and Beautiful Areas in the City

There are peaceful areas of calm within Heidelberg's bustling vitality that tempt tourists to unwind. A peaceful refuge where you may connect with nature and find inner tranquility, these serene gardens and picturesque areas offer a break from the bustle of the city.

- **The picturesque Schlossgarten (Castle Garden)** is one of the city's most cherished green areas. This vast park, which is at the foot of Heidelberg Castle, is home to blossoming flower beds, verdant meadows, and charming pathways. Explore the garden at your own pace, find some shade under a tree, or relax on a bench with a view of the Neckar River. Enjoy the enticing aromas, the calming sounds of nature, and the expansive views of the castle and the surrounding area.

- **The English Garden (Englischer Garten)** is a well-kept secret within the Schlossgarten. With its well-kept lawns, winding walks, and colorful blossoms, this delightful garden is a haven of peace. Find quiet spots where you may relax with a book, have a picnic, or just take in the beauty of your surroundings. The English Garden, a favorite hangout for both locals and tourists, provides a tranquil haven from the busy metropolis.

- **A Buddhist Chinese Garden** called the Buddhist Chinese Garden may be found next to the Heidelberg Zoo if you're looking for a little Zen. With tranquil ponds, delicately arched bridges, and meticulously maintained gardens, this tranquil paradise is modeled by traditional Chinese gardens. Enjoy the splendor of this serene hideaway by taking a leisurely stroll around the twisting trails, seeing the elaborate pavilions, and finding calm.

- **The Neckarwiese** is another picturesque location that mesmerizes with its natural beauty. This vast riverfront park offers a magnificent environment for leisurely strolls, picnics, or outdoor activities as it spans along the Neckar River's banks. Take in some peace and quiet by the water's side, bask in the sunshine on the grassy banks, or play a friendly game of football or frisbee with your pals. The Neckarwiese is a well-liked gathering spot for residents where you can enjoy the tranquil ambiance while taking in the river's gentle flow.

- Visit the **Philosophengärtchen (Philosophers' Garden),** which is located on the Heiligenberg hillside a short distance from the city center. This undiscovered treasure provides a tranquil haven and rewards guests with breath-taking panoramas of Heidelberg. Choose a space on a bench and take in the calm of the surroundings while you sit and take in the expansive views of the city, the river, and the lush surroundings.

Heidelberg's quiet gardens and picturesque locations offer a peaceful haven in the heart of the cityscape.

These hidden sanctuaries provide a refuge of calm whether you're looking for a quiet opportunity to ponder, a beautiful setting for a leisurely walk, or simply a spot to relax and recharge.

Accept the wonder of nature, let your concerns float away, and allow Heidelberg's tranquil gardens and natural areas to renew your spirit.

4. IMMERSION IN HISTORY AND CULTURE

Heidelberg is a city rich in culture and history, where each building preserves a piece of the city's past. Discover the fascinating city's rich history by visiting its historical sites, learning about its cultural riches, and participating in its thriving artistic community.

Start your adventure at Heidelberg Castle, a recognizable representation of the grandeur and history of the city. This magnificent fortification dominates the Königstuhl hill, providing views of the charming Old Town and the Neckar River.

Admire the magnificent architecture as you stroll through the castle grounds, including the Friedrich Building's Gothic façade and the commanding Great Vat ruins.

Enter the castle's interior to see the **enormous wine barrel known as the Heidelberg Tun and the German Pharmacy Museum,**

both of which are listed in the Guinness Book of World Records. Enjoy sweeping views of the city, the river, and the surrounding countryside from the castle's terraces as you step back in time to a time of knights and aristocracy.

Heidelberg's rich tradition and artistic energy can be experienced by immersing yourself in the city's history and culture. Each encounter provides a window into the past and the present, deepening your understanding of Heidelberg's distinctive cultural tapestry.

Examples include touring historic castles, taking a stroll through the eerie Old Town, or participating in the city's bustling arts scene. So embrace the allure of history and culture, let the tales unfold in front of you, and set out on a discovery quest in this magical city.

4.1   A Peep Into the Interesting Past of Heidelberg

With a more than 800-year history, Heidelberg has a fascinating past that entices tourists to explore its enthralling tales and impressive heritage. Take a trip through time as we find hints of Heidelberg's fascinating past and the historical influences that still influence the city today.

The story opens with the establishment of Heidelberg University in 1386, one of Germany's first institutions and a major force in the development of the city's intellectual and cultural life. Heidelberg attracted academics from all over Europe, which helped to establish its standing as a hub of learning. Feel the echoes of centuries of academic endeavor as you stroll through the lovely campus, which is decorated with antique buildings and charming courtyards.

Heidelberg Castle, the city's most recognizable landmark, is a reminder of its opulence and stormy past.

It was initially constructed in the 13th century as a castle and over time transformed into a spectacular Renaissance palace. The castle, however, was destroyed and burned, leaving behind an intriguing mixture of remains and architectural relics. Investigate the courtyards, towers, and gardens of the castle, envisioning the majesty that once filled these walls, and awe at the tenacity that has kept it beautiful.

The Old Town (Altstadt) of Heidelberg transports visitors back to the Middle Ages thanks to its winding streets, restored buildings, and extensive history. As you wander through its narrow, cobblestone streets, you will come upon Heidelberg's Church of the Holy Spirit, which serves as both a representation of the city and a record of its political and theological evolution. Consider the centuries of worship and the transformation of the city as you ascend the tower to take in the panoramic views.

A trip over the Alte Brücke provides a window into Heidelberg's former prominence as a center of trade and commerce.

For more than 250 years, the city has been connected by this charming bridge that spans the Neckar River and is embellished with statues. As you gaze in awe at the scenery, consider the hive of activity that once characterized this crucial thoroughfare for passengers and traders.

A trip to the Palatinate Museum is necessary to comprehend the historical significance of Heidelberg in its entirety. The museum, which is housed in a beautiful structure, displays objects and exhibits that explore the history of the city, from its Roman foundations to its position as a key political hub in the Electoral Palatinate. Admire the archaeological discoveries, art collections, and historical items that vividly depict Heidelberg's complex past.

Heidelberg's intriguing past infuses the city's culture and traditions as well as its famous landmarks. Heidelberg's historical heritage is integrated into its modern character, from the vibrant student culture that the university fosters to the lasting enthusiasm for literature and the arts.

Allow yourself to be taken to a bygone period as you visit Heidelberg, where the tales of emperors, scholars, and common people converge.

You are invited to explore the city's intriguing past, marvel at its architectural wonders, and learn more about the factors that have formed Heidelberg into the alluring destination it is today.

Immerse yourself in history, follow in the footsteps of history, and let Heidelberg's intriguing past fascinate you.

4.2   Putting Heidelberg's Art and History on Display through Museums, Galleries and Exhibitions

Heidelberg is a cultural center with an abundance of museums, galleries, and exhibitions in addition to its beautiful surroundings and compelling architecture.

Explore these educational institutions that highlight the creativity, legacy, and stories of Heidelberg and beyond to immerse yourself in the worlds of art and history.

The Kurpfälzisches Museum (Palatinate Museum) is a veritable gold mine of art and history. This museum transports visitors through time, from the ancient period to the present, and is housed in a historic building.

Learn about Heidelberg's ancient past through archeological discoveries, marvel at medieval sculptures and religious relics, and become immersed in the rich history of the Palatinate region.

Masterpieces from a variety of eras are included in the museum's art collection, including Renaissance paintings, Baroque sculptures, and modern pieces. Each exhibit provides an enthralling look into Heidelberg's and the area's cultural past.

- **Heidelberger Kunstverein (Heidelberg Art Association):** This gallery of modern art presents provocative shows by national and international artists. Utilize a variety of media, such as paintings, sculptures, installations, and multimedia works, to embrace the diversity of artistic expressions. The constantly shifting exhibits push boundaries, provoke debate, and showcase Heidelberg's thriving creative community. Engage with the artworks, go to events and presentations by the artists, and allow the creativity to move you and get you thinking.

- **The Carl Bosch Museum:** It offers a distinctive perspective on Heidelberg's industrial past. This museum, which is housed in the Nobel laureate Carl Bosch's former home, examines the creative accomplishments and contributions of the chemical industry. Learn about the important discoveries Bosch and his team made that changed industry and helped to create the modern world. The tale of scientific advancement is brought to life through interesting displays, interactive exhibitions, and historical artifacts, emphasizing Heidelberg's contribution to the advancement of science and industry.

- **Museum of the Palatinate:** Visit to discover the fascinating realm of natural history. This extensive museum offers a variety of displays that explore the region's zoological, botanical, and geological characteristics. The museum offers an immersive experience that informs and inspires, with everything from prehistoric fossils and minerals to elaborate taxidermy displays and multimedia presentations. Learn about the ecosystems that surround Heidelberg, experience the wonders of nature, and develop a greater respect for the environment.

- **The Druckladen im Zwinger** is a must-see for everyone who is interested in the history of printing. This printing workshop is located inside the Zwinger, a historic structure, and it features traditional printing methods and bookbinding craftsmanship. Watch accomplished craftspeople at work as they produce stunning handcrafted books and demonstrate letterpress printing. Find out how printing has changed over time and how important it is for preserving cultural heritage and spreading knowledge.

There are many possibilities to immerse oneself in the worlds of art and history in Heidelberg through its museums, galleries, and exhibitions. These institutions appeal to a variety of interests and offer a greater understanding of

Heidelberg's cultural landscape, whether you're enthralled by historical treasures, moved by modern pieces of art, or intrigued by scientific advancements.

Therefore, set out on an exploratory adventure, extend your perspectives, and allow creativity and storytelling flow as you interact with Heidelberg's art and history.

4.3 Heidelberg Festivals and Cultural Events to Attend

The city of Heidelberg comes to life all year long with a thriving calendar of festivals and cultural events. These events offer a chance to become immersed in the local culture, observe customs, and make priceless memories. They range from exhilarating street parades to exquisite musical concerts.

Find out about Heidelberg's fascinating festivals and cultural events.

- **The Heidelberg Castle Illuminations, also known as**

Heidelberg Schlossbeleuchtung, are one of the city's most recognizable events. This magnificent light show, which occurs multiple times a year, turns Heidelberg Castle into a spellbinding backdrop. As night falls, thousands of fireworks light up the castle and its surroundings, creating an amazing show that can be seen for miles. Locals and tourists alike are drawn to the event, which includes music, to experience this entrancing blend of light, sound, and history.

- One of the most important events on the cultural calendar is the **Heidelberg Spring Festival (Heidelberger Frühling).** This well-known music event features a wide variety of acts, such as classical concerts, chamber music, and experimental music. Internationally renowned musicians congregate in Heidelberg to showcase their extraordinary skills while mesmerizing audiences with their brilliance and artistry. The Heidelberg Spring Festival offers a rich and encompassing musical experience, ranging from private recitals in revered spaces to opulent symphonic performances.

- **The Heidelberg Literature Festival (Heidelberger Literaturtage)** is a must-attend event for bookworms. Renowned writers, poets, and thinkers come together for this literary extravaganza's series of readings, panel discussions, and workshops. Explore the world of literature, participate in stimulating discussions, and find fresh literary voices at this exciting and motivating event.

- The renowned theater festival **Heidelberger Stückemarkt** honors modern playwriting and performance. This event, which presents cutting-edge and original theatrical works, draws theater lovers and professionals from all over the world.
  Discover provocative plays, avant-garde performances, and lively debates that

push the limits of theater and showcase the variety of artistic expression.

- **The Heidelberg Castle Festival (Heidelberger Schlossfestspiele)** is the main event of the summer. This outdoor festival offers a schedule of theater, music, and dance events against the backdrop of the castle ruins. With everything from ballet and jazz concerts to classical plays and operas, the festival presents a special chance to take in top-notch acts in a genuinely wonderful environment.

The Old Town of Heidelberg is enchanted by the joyful scent of mulled wine, roasted chestnuts, and gingerbread at the annual Weihnachtsmarkt celebration.

Browse the quaint booths festooned with holiday decorations, indulge in regional specialties, and discover one-of-a-kind presents for your loved ones.
Live music, carolers, and other forms of entertainment are also present at the market,

fostering a festive ambiance that perfectly captures the spirit of the Christmas season.

The colorful traditions, artistic expressions, and festive atmosphere of Heidelberg are on display at these festivals and cultural events. These celebrations offer a special chance to engage with the local community, experience the cultural heritage, and make priceless memories.

Whether you're taking in a mesmerizing light show at the castle, immersing yourself in the world of music and literature, or enjoying the festive delights of the Christmas Market.

Therefore, schedule your trip to coincide with these exciting events, soak up the positive energy, and let Heidelberg's festivals and cultural events enchant your senses.

5. LOCAL CUISINE AND CULINARY DELIGHTS

Heidelberg is a city full of architectural marvels, cultural activities, and a culinary paradise that attracts foodies from all over the world. Explore the culinary delicacies and regional cuisine that make Heidelberg a true food lover's dream as we embark on a culinary trip.

Heidelberg's food scene is a tasteful fusion of regional specialties, foreign influences, and cutting-edge culinary inventions.

Explore the varied selection of restaurants and cafes in Heidelberg to taste the colorful foreign flavors of the city. There are many options to suit every palate, ranging from quaint cafés and bistros to elegant eating places.

Enjoy delicious pasta meals made in Italy with fresh, regional ingredients, or taste the flavorful spices and aromas of Middle Eastern or Indian food.

Innovative restaurants combine international influences with regional ingredients to create one-of-a-kind and delectable dishes for people looking for a synthesis of culinary traditions.

The Neckar River runs through Heidelberg, providing opportunities to enjoy delectable fresh fish dishes. The flavors of the river come alive as you savor a platter of grilled salmon or a supper of smoked trout by the river, taking you to a world of gourmet bliss.

Heidelberg offers a vast selection of mouthwatering desserts and sweets to sate your hunger. Try the renowned Studentenkuss (student's kiss), a popular local treat made of marzipan and wrapped in chocolate since the 19th century.

Enjoy a piece of the famous Obstkuchen fruit tart from the area, which features a buttery crust and a variety of seasonal fruits. And don't forget to treat yourself to some creamy, velvety Spaghettieis, a fun ice cream delicacy that looks like a plate of spaghetti.

Explore the colorful markets in Heidelberg where you can get a wide variety of fresh produce, artisanal cheeses, cured meats, and other foods to improve your gastronomic experience.

You may fully experience the tastes and fragrances of the area by perusing the lovely selection of local goods available at the Wochenmarkt (weekly market) in the center of the Old Town.

Enjoy an outdoor meal in one of Heidelberg's beautiful parks or gardens while interacting with friendly sellers, learning about new ingredients, and gathering provisions for a picnic.

Enjoy some of the regional libations Heidelberg has to offer to go along with your gastronomic explorations.
At one of the classic beer gardens, sip on a glass of locally brewed beer or savor some of the superb wines produced in the area, particularly the Riesling variety that thrives in the nearby vineyards.

Wine lovers can even take a wine tour to see the charming vineyards and wineries tucked away in the nearby hills.

The native cuisine and culinary treats in Heidelberg are a feast for the senses, encapsulating the unique tastes, customs, and ingenuity of the area from customary German fare to the city's diversified culinary scene making sure that every palate is satiated with foreign fusion cuisine.

So have a culinary adventure, enjoy the flavors, and let Heidelberg's culinary gems enchant and delight you.

5.1 Indulging in regional delicacies and typical German Cuisine

The city of Heidelberg is proud of its illustrious culinary history and offers a delectable selection of traditional German meals and regional delicacies.

Enjoy the hearty, reassuring, and occasionally unexpected gastronomic delights that characterize German food as you immerse yourself in the regional flavors.

- **The Renowned Schnitzel** is a traditional German delicacy that you must have while visiting Heidelberg. These soft and crispy meat dishes—whether it's Wiener Schnitzel (breaded and fried veal cutlet) or Jägerschnitzel (pork or chicken cutlet with mushroom sauce)—are cherished classics. Schnitzel is a filling and flavorful meal when served with a side of warm potato salad or sautéed potatoes.

- **Sauerbraten**, a robust and flavorful dish, is another must-try. Typically made from beef, this traditional pot roast is slow-cooked to perfection after being marinated for many days in a solution of vinegar, water, and spices. The outcome is juicy, soft meat that has absorbed the marinade's acidic and aromatic tastes. Sauerbraten displays the richness and complexity of German cuisine when it is served with a side of red cabbage and potato dumplings.

- Heidelberg provides delicacies like **Maultaschen**, a Swabian dish resembling dumplings or ravioli and stuffed with a blend of minced pork, spinach, and herbs, for those looking for a taste of regional specialties. These mouthwatering packets of taste are frequently served with a hearty portion of thick gravy and a side of crisp lettuce or sautéed veggies.

- Try the traditional **German potato soup**, also known as **Kartoffelsuppe**, if you enjoy substantial soups. With potatoes, onions, bacon, and a variety of herbs and spices, this creamy and warming soup is produced, and you won't be able to stop at just one bowl.

- Germany has a solid reputation when it comes to bread. You may try a variety of **freshly made bread** in Heidelberg, including the perennially famous pretzels. These doughy knots are twisted and dusted with coarse salt. They have the perfect amount of chewiness and softness. For a truly authentic culinary experience, serve them with classic German sausages or enjoy them as a snack on their own.

- Discover the world of German delicacies and pastries to sate your sweet taste. Enjoy a slice of **Black Forest Cake (Schwarzwälder Kirschtorte),** a rich chocolate cake infused with Kirsch (cherry brandy) and covered with whipped cream and cherries. Apfelstrudel, a wonderful apple-filled pastry served warm with a coating of powdered sugar and a dollop of vanilla sauce or ice cream, is another sweet delicacy to try.

Grab a local beer or wine to go along with your culinary tour of Heidelberg.

You may discover a wide selection of traditional brews in Germany, from light and crisp Pilsners to malty and rich Dunkels. Germany is known for its beer culture.

The culinary scene in Heidelberg is full with regional delicacies and classic German meals that showcase the history, culture, and flavors of the area.

So take advantage of the chance to indulge in these delectable treats, discover the neighborhood's markets and eateries, and allow Heidelberg's traditional German cuisine's flavors carry you away to a world of savory satisfaction.

5.2 Restaurant suggestions for Authentic Culinary Experiences

For those looking for authentic culinary experiences, Heidelberg offers a wide variety of dining options. The city takes pride in its diversified gastronomic environment.

Every appetite can be satisfied by the city's diverse food scene, which offers everything from classic German fare to international fusion cuisine.

Here are some eating suggestions for real and unforgettable gastronomic experiences to help you traverse the culinary joys of Heidelberg.

1. The Old Town of Heidelberg: This is home to the famous Zum Guldenen Schaf, which offers traditional German cuisine with a contemporary touch. Take pleasure in regional favorites like roasted pork knuckle, sausages with sauerkraut, and handmade spaetzle. A very enjoyable experience, dining at Zum Guldenen Schaf is made possible by the welcoming ambiance and excellent service.

2. Schnitzelbank: This is a sanctuary for schnitzel aficionados, as the name of the restaurant suggests. Schnitzelbank, a restaurant close to the Neckar River, serves a wide range of schnitzel selections, including inventive varieties like the Jägerschnitzel with a mushroom and cheese topping in addition to the classic Wiener Schnitzel. A delicious and genuine German dining experience is guaranteed by the substantial quantities and savory accompaniments.

3. Vetter's Alt Heidelberger Brauhaus: Since 1671, has been a popular dining and drinking establishment for both locals and tourists. Vetter's Alt Heidelberger Brauhaus is a must-visit for beer connoisseurs and food lovers alike because of its authentic German beer and substantial fare. Try their world-famous Vetter 33 beer, one of the strongest in the world, and serve it with traditional fare like sauerkraut, sausages, and pork knuckle.

4. Kulturbrauerei: Housed in a historic brewery, this restaurant provides a distinctive eating experience in a bustling setting. This brewpub offers a variety of craft beers to go along with their varied cuisine by fusing traditional brewing methods with a contemporary touch. Eat traditional German fare like bratwurst, potato pancakes, and pretzels while taking in the lively atmosphere and live music of the restaurant.

5. Hemingway Lounge: A top pick for a taste of international food with a dash of sophistication. This upmarket restaurant specializes in fusion cuisine, fusing regional ingredients with flavors from around the globe. Hemingway Lounge provides a sophisticated dining experience in a fashionable environment, with everything from exquisite steaks and seafood delicacies to vegetarian and vegan options.

6. Marstall: Marstall, a unique dining experience with breathtaking city views, is situated inside the grounds of Heidelberg Castle. By using fresh, in-season ingredients from nearby farmers and producers, this restaurant highlights the regional flavors in its food. A wonderful experience, dining at Marstall is made possible by the exquisite setting and expansive views.

7. Die Kurfürstenstube: This is a renowned restaurant known for its superb meals and opulent ambiance. It is housed within the historic Hotel Zum Ritter St. Georg.

The inventive and painstakingly prepared dishes at this Michelin-starred restaurant highlight the finest in local and global cuisine. Die Kurfürstenstube is a great option for a special occasion or a memorable dining experience because of its attentive service and sophisticated culinary options.

8. Markthalle Heidelberg: If you want a more relaxed eating experience or to learn about regional ingredients. A wide range of food stalls and sellers can be found in this bustling food hall, selling everything from fresh fruit and gourmet cheeses to sweet sweets and international street cuisine. Eat, try new cuisines, and take in the buzzing ambiance of this gastronomic mecca.

These restaurant suggestions offer a sense of Heidelberg's varied culinary scene and a selection of real experiences to satisfy every taste and inclination.

These restaurants guarantee a memorable and tasty eating experience in Heidelberg, whether you're looking for classic German food, fusion cuisine, or cosmopolitan cuisines.

5.3 Enjoying Delicious Local Brews at Beer Gardens

One of the finest ways to really experience Heidelberg's centuries-old beer culture is to visit the city's beer gardens and try some of the regional brews. Here is a thorough and well-organized reference to beer gardens and local beers in Heidelberg, covering everything from ancient places to lively outdoor areas.

- **Heidelberger Schlossquell:** is a well-known beer garden with breathtaking views of the city that is close to Heidelberg Castle. You can have a cool pint of their specialty beer, Heidelberger Schlossquell Pilsner, which is renowned for its crisp and pure flavor, here.

  Enjoy the relaxed ambiance that perfectly encapsulates the beer garden experience while lounging beneath the shade of chestnut trees and mingling with locals and guests alike.

- **Kulturbrauerei:** Located in a former brewery, Kulturbrauerei is a brewpub that blends old-world charm with modern ambiance. Try some of their artisan beers, which are locally brewed utilizing time-honored techniques and premium ingredients. Kulturbrauerei offers a variety of beers to suit every taste, from light and refreshing lagers to hoppy IPAs and malty ales. Enjoy your drink with delectable pub fare while taking in the lively atmosphere of this well-liked establishment.

- **Stadtketten:** Beer connoisseurs should visit Stadtketten, a hidden gem located in Heidelberg's Old Town. This microbrewery specializes in producing artisanal, small-batch beers utilizing ingredients that are found locally. The beer selection at Stadtketten is broad and always changing, ranging from experimental brews to classic German varieties like Hefeweizen and Dunkel.

Enjoy their creations in a warm and welcoming environment while chatting with the enthusiastic brewers who are willing to impart their skills.

- **Brauhaus Vetter:** is a wonderful brewery and restaurant in Heidelberg that offers a variety of unique brews that enchant the palate. **Try their Vetter's 33 Export Lager, one of the strongest beers in the world according to the Guinness World Records.** A welcoming environment is created for you to enjoy your beer-drinking experience by the warm ambient, the rustic decor, and the helpful personnel.

- **The Neckar River's Neckar Kulturbrauerei Schwetzinger Terrasse:** provides a magnificent environment for sipping a refreshing beverage. The Kulturbrauerei Schwetzinger Terrasse is the perfect place to unwind with its large outdoor seating space and breathtaking river views.

A variety of locally brewed beers are available, including seasonal specials, crisp wheat beers, and light lagers.

- **Perkeo-Garten:** is a lovely beer garden in the center of Heidelberg's Old Town that has the name of the fabled court jester of Heidelberg Castle. This welcoming establishment offers a selection of domestic and imported beers and offers a relaxed setting where you may meet locals and other tourists. Enjoy a nice beer, take in the welcoming atmosphere, and revel in the conviviality that beer brings.

It is a must-do activity when visiting Heidelberg to stroll through the city's beer gardens and try the regional brews. These suggestions provide a variety of opportunities to explore Heidelberg's beer culture and enjoy the distinctive flavors of the area, from historic locations to secret jewels.

Let's toast to a fun day drinking beer in Heidelberg!

6. OUTSIDE ACTIVITIES

Heidelberg provides a wide range of outdoor excursions for nature lovers and thrill seekers in addition to its rich cultural and historical legacy.

Here is a full and comprehensive reference to the outdoor adventures Heidelberg has to offer, from scenic treks to exhilarating water sports.

Heidelberg has much to offer everyone looking to connect with nature, discover historical places, and embrace exhilarating experiences thanks to its wide variety of outdoor activities.

Experience the splendor of nature up close and make lifelong memories in this captivating city.

6.1 Exploring the Parks, Gardens, and Natural Beauties of Heidelberg

Heidelberg is renowned for its extensive green areas, parks, and gardens that highlight the city's natural beauty in addition to its rich historical and cultural attractions.

Here is a complete and comprehensive guide to seeing Heidelberg's natural beauties, from well-kept gardens to vast parks.

1. Schlossgarten

This is a magnificent park with beautiful views of the city and the Neckar River that is close to Heidelberg Castle. This nicely maintained park has well-kept lawns, colorful flower beds, and shady walks that are lined with trees. Enjoy a leisurely stroll, a quiet place to unwind, or a picnic while admiring the magnificent surroundings.

2. The Heidelberg University Botanical Garden

This is a paradise for people who are interested in plants.

It is located on the university's Neuenheimer Feld campus. This four-hectare botanical haven is home to a wide variety of plants from all over the world. Visit themed areas like the Alpine Garden, Mediterranean Garden, and Tropical Greenhouse to see a wide array of rare and exotic plants.

3. Neckarwiese
Situated on the Neckar River's banks, Neckarwiese is a sizable riverfront park where residents and guests congregate to unwind, play sports, and take part in outdoor activities. Open grass, shady trees, and grilling spots can be found in this vast green area. Rent a bike, go on a picnic, or just relax while taking in the tranquil setting and expansive views of the river and the city.

4. Philosophenweg
Climb the Philosopher's Walk, a picturesque path that meanders around the Heiligenberg Mountain's slopes. Beautiful views of Heidelberg's Old Town, the Neckar River, and the surrounding hills may be seen from this beautiful path.

You'll see why this location has served as inspiration for poets and philosophers throughout history as you stroll amid terraced vineyards and old-growth forests.

5. Botanischer Garten der Universität Heidelberg

This floral haven is located in the Neuenheim neighborhood and is yet another to discover. A broad variety of plant species, including attractive, medicinal, and tropical plants, can be found in this botanical garden. Enjoy the tranquil atmosphere by taking a leisurely stroll through the themed gardens, like the Systematic Garden and the Rock Garden.

6. Kurpfalz-Park

Just outside of Heidelberg, Kurpfalz-Park offers a fun outdoor activity for the whole family. This wildlife and amusement park provides the ideal fusion of fun and the outdoors. Discover domestic and foreign animals, exhilarating attractions, and themed zones like the Adventure Playground and Dinosaur Park. A pleasant day spent surrounded by nature can be had here.

7. Tiergarten Heidelberg

Tiergarten Heidelberg is a wonderful wildlife park that shelters a variety of native species. It is located in the Neckarhäuserhof neighborhood. Explore the forest trails, spot deer, wild boars, and other native animals in their natural settings, and discover the region's efforts to conserve biodiversity. The park is a well-liked location for families because it also has a petting zoo and picnic spots.

8. Theodor-Heuss-Anlage

This sizable urban park, which is close to the city's heart, offers a peaceful retreat from the busy city. This lush haven has wide open lawns, strolling lanes, and lovely flowerbeds. Take a leisurely stroll, have a picnic, or just unwind on a bench and take in the tranquil atmosphere.

9. Bruchsee

Located not far from Heidelberg, Bruchsee is a charming lake surrounded by verdant vegetation. Given the availability of swimming, boating, and fishing options, it's the perfect location for nature enthusiasts.

Walk along the lakeshore, hire a paddleboat, or just take in the tranquil atmosphere of this natural wonder.

Heidelberg's parks, gardens, and outdoor areas offer a respite from the city's bustle and an opportunity to appreciate nature.

Discovering these green retreats will leave you refreshed and inspired by Heidelberg's natural beauty, whether you're looking for relaxation, outdoor activities, or a picturesque getaway.

6.2 Local Trails for Biking, Hiking, and Other Outdoor Pursuits

Heidelberg is a gateway to breathtaking natural landscapes and outdoor adventures in addition to being a city rich in history and culture.

Heidelberg provides a wealth of chances for hiking, riding, and participating in numerous outdoor sports due to its closeness to the Odenwald Forest, the Neckar River, and lovely nearby towns.

Here is a thorough guide that will help you explore Heidelberg's surroundings in search of adventure.

1. Hiking in the Odenwald Forest: Do wear your hiking boots and explore the magnificent pathways of Heidelberg's surrounding lush paradise, the Odenwald Forest. The forest has a variety of hiking trails that are appropriate for hikers of all levels, from easy strolls to strenuous mountain hikes. As you immerse yourself in the area's natural splendor, find secret waterfalls, historic castles, and sweeping vistas.

2. Neckar Valley Cycle Path: Rent a bike and ride the picturesque Neckar Valley Cycle Path, a clearly signposted path that follows the Neckar River's meandering course. Ride your bike through quaint villages, wineries, and verdant countryside as you take in the stunning scenery. From Heidelberg to Mannheim, there is a cycle path that allows you to travel at your own leisure while discovering the area.

3. Water Sports on the Neckar River: Lovers of water sports have a playground in the Neckar River. Hire a kayak, canoe, or stand-up paddleboard and explore the river's calm currents. Enjoy the peace and quiet, witness the wildlife, and discover Heidelberg's calm beauty from a fresh angle.

4. Mountain biking in the Odenwald: The Odenwald region has exhilarating mountain biking paths for thrill seekers. Ride through rocky terrain, overcome difficult ascents, and take pleasure in spectacular descents. Mountain bikers of all skill levels have the perfect playground in the Odenwald's various terrain.

5. Rock climbing in the Pfalz: The Pfalz region, noted for its rock formations and good climbing opportunities, is a short drive from Heidelberg. Put your climbing equipment on and try out your talents on the stunning sandstone cliffs. There are routes available to suit all skill levels, whether you're a novice or an expert climber.

6. Adventure Parks: The area around Heidelberg is home to various adventure parks if you're traveling with family or looking for a fun-filled day of adventure. For guests of all ages, these parks provide thrilling activities including zip lines, obstacle courses, and other thrilling experiences.

7. Visiting Neighboring Towns: Escape the metropolis and visit the quaint nearby towns and villages that surround Heidelberg. These picturesque locations provide chances for leisurely strolls, seeing historic buildings, and taking in the peace and quiet of the countryside. Among the wonderful towns just waiting to be found are Ladenburg, Schwetzingen, and Speyer.

8. Species Observation: The area surrounding Heidelberg is filled with a variety of species, making it a fantastic vacation spot for outdoors enthusiasts. Visit parks and nature reserves, like the Schwetzinger Hardt Nature Reserve, to see different bird species, deer, and other local wildlife in their natural settings.

9. Tours of the Vineyards: Take this opportunity to explore the vineyards that surround Heidelberg. Take a guided tour to explore the beautiful vineyards, discover how wine is made, and enjoy wine tastings. Immerse yourself in the local cuisine and cultural treasures.

A variety of outdoor activities are available in Heidelberg and the surrounding areas, catering to the interests of all adventurers. There are various ways to appreciate nature's beauty and have exhilarating adventures, from relaxing hikes to heart-pounding riding paths, from water sports to rock climbing.

So grab your kit, enjoy the great outdoors, and use Heidelberg's surroundings as your playground for exciting outdoor adventures.

6.3   Watersports and Cruises on the Neckar River

Heidelberg's Neckar River provides a magnificent backdrop and a singular viewpoint of the city's splendor as it flows gracefully through the historic center.

You may fully immerse yourself in the picturesque surroundings while taking in the beauty and appeal of Heidelberg from a fresh perspective by setting off on a Neckar River cruise or partaking in water sports. Here is a thorough and in-depth guide to Heidelberg's Neckar River cruises and water sports.

- **Take a leisurely Neckar River ride by boarding one of the lovely riverboats available.** Experience sweeping views of Heidelberg's iconic Heidelberg Castle, the Old Bridge, and the charming Old Town. As you float around the calm waters, listen to engrossing narration about the city's history and architecture. Several other types of cruises are available, such as sightseeing cruises, sunset cruises, and themed tours that highlight the natural beauty of the river and its surrounds.

- **Rent a canoe or kayak and paddle down the Neckar River at your own pace for a more active water excursion.** Discover the peaceful stretches of the river, make your way through mild rapids, and take in the tranquility of the natural surroundings. By exploring secluded areas and taking in the natural beauty of the riverbanks, canoeing and kayaking offer a singular opportunity to come closer to the water and experience a sense of freedom.

- **Stand-Up Paddleboarding (SUP).** The Neckar River is a great place to attempt this thrilling water sport, which has grown in popularity in recent years. A full-body workout and a distinctive view of Heidelberg may be had by standing on a paddleboard and using a paddle to glide over the water.

The tranquil waters of the Neckar offer a safe and comfortable setting for paddleboarding, whether you're a novice or an expert.

- **Exploring the riverfront promenades and parks along the Neckar River** is a wonderful opportunity to take advantage of the closeness to the water, even though it is not a water activity in and of itself. Relax on benches or go for a leisurely bike ride along the riverbanks. You may even have a picnic in the parks. The promenades allow you to take in the tranquil atmosphere and make connections with nature while providing magnificent views of the river and the town.

- **Fishing.** The Neckar River offers anglers the chance to participate in their pastime. Try your luck casting a line and catching trout, pike, and perch, among other fish species. Please make sure you have the required fishing licenses and abide by local laws.

- While not technically a water activity, dining or drinking at one of the many riverfront cafés and restaurants is an excellent opportunity to take in the ambience of the Neckar River. Select a restaurant with outside seating so you may enjoy delicious food while taking in the view of the river and its surroundings.

- **Photography and sketching. With** its picturesque scenery and architectural marvels, the Neckar River offers photographers and artists a motivating backdrop. Photograph or draw Heidelberg's lovely riverbanks, bridges, and surface reflections to capture the essence of the city's appeal. Let the Neckar's peaceful beauty inspire your imagination.

- **Riverfront Events and Festivals** Throughout the year, the Neckar River will host a number of noteworthy events and festivals. The riverbanks come alive with vivid celebrations that offer tourists a one-of-a-kind and unforgettable experience, ranging from music festivals and open-air concerts to cultural celebrations and fireworks displays.

You can see Heidelberg's splendor from a fresh angle by setting out on a Neckar River tour or engaging in water sports.

The Neckar River guarantees a wonderful and enchanted experience for everyone who ventures upon its gentle currents, whether you prefer to take a leisurely cruise, paddle your way through the water, or simply enjoy the river's ambience.

7. DAY TRIPS FROM HEIDELBERG

Heidelberg is a fascinating city in its own right, but it also makes a great starting point for trips outside of the city. There are many day trip alternatives that offer a change of scenery and the ability to explore further into the rich cultural and historical legacy of the area, from beautiful villages to breathtaking natural surroundings. The following is a thorough and in-depth guide on day trips from Heidelberg.

From Heidelberg, you can take a day excursion to explore the area's rich history, scenic beauty, and cultural riches.

The surrounding surroundings provide a variety of experiences that will improve your trip to Heidelberg, whether you decide to explore lovely villages, immerse yourself in nature, or indulge in gastronomic delights.

7.1 Discovering the Charms of Area Towns and Villages: Going Beyond Heidelberg

There are other adjacent towns and villages that are just waiting to be explored, so Heidelberg's appeal goes well beyond its city borders. Each place has its own character that offers a window into the people, their history, and their beautiful surroundings.

These adjacent towns and villages provide a lovely getaway from the hustle and bustle of Heidelberg, whether you're looking for small-town charm, spectacular architecture, or unspoiled natural beauty.

Here is a thorough guide on visiting local cities and villages that is well-detailed.

1. Ladenburg: This little-known city with a fascinating past is close to Heidelberg. Its well-preserved medieval old town will transport you back in time as you explore its winding cobblestone lanes, half-timbered homes, and lovely squares.

Explore the Roman ruins, which include a Roman theater and a Roman villa, to learn more about the town's automotive history. Alternatively, visit the Carl Benz Museum. Additionally, Ladenburg has lovely riverfront promenades that offer a tranquil ambiance for leisurely strolls.

2. Schwetzingen: A short distance from Heidelberg is the town of Schwetzingen, which offers a lovely fusion of culture and environment. The magnificent Schwetzingen Palace and Gardens, a masterpiece of Baroque architecture encircled by sizable landscaped gardens, are the town's most well-known landmarks. Discover the elaborate fountains, statues, and geometric patterns that embellish the grounds while taking in the palace's lavish interiors. A yearly music festival is also held in Schwetzingen, drawing well-known musicians from all over the world.

3. Dilsberg: is a lovely medieval village with a long history, perched on a hilltop with a view of the Neckar River.

Enjoy the beautiful ambiance by taking a leisurely stroll through its winding streets adorned with half-timbered homes. Visit Dilsberg Castle, a fortification that has been restored and offers sweeping views of the surrounding area. The hamlet provides stunning vistas, inviting eateries, and a serene ambiance that urges you to relax and get away from the bustle of city life.

4. Eberbach: A town famous for its historic monastery and vineyards, Eberbach is tucked away in the Neckar Valley. The spectacular Eberbach Abbey, a former Cistercian abbey from the 12th century, is well worth seeing. Admire the cloister, the cathedral, and the wine cellar's Romanesque and Gothic architecture for their splendor. In addition to providing possibilities for wine tastings and vineyard tours, Eberbach serves as a gateway to the wine area.

5. Neckargemünd: is a lovely town with a charming medieval town center that is located at the meeting point of the Neckar and Elsenz rivers. Explore the streets of this quaint city, which are lined with enticing cafes and colorful half-timber buildings. The "Alte Brücke," a medieval bridge in the town with beautiful views of the river and the hills in the distance, is a well-known landmark. Don't pass up the chance to climb the adjacent Dilsberg Castle for sweeping views.

6. Schriesheim: This picturesque village, which is surrounded by vineyards and undulating hills, provides the ideal fusion of nature and culture. Discover the lovely market square and well-preserved half-timbered homes that make up the medieval town core. The town is particularly well-known for the charming Schriesheim Castle castle ruins, which make for a beautiful setting for nature hikes and expansive views of the surrounding countryside.

7. Weinheim: also referred to as the "Two Castle Town," is a bustling city with a rich architectural history. Visit the majestic Dom and explore the medieval Marktplatz with its vibrant half-timbered homes.

Explore the exquisitely designed Exotenwald, a botanical park that is home to a broad range of exotic trees, and Weinheim Castle. Additionally, there are options for dining, shopping, and taking part in regional festivities in the town.

8. Neckarsteinach: is a lovely town along the Neckar River that is well-known for its four castle ruins. Hike up to each castle for sweeping views of the river valley, or take a boat ride along the river to observe the castles from a different angle. Nature lovers and history buffs can both find peace in Neckarsteinach's picturesque backdrop of vineyards and lush vegetation.

9. Speyer: Traveling to this ancient city is like traveling back in time. Speyer, which is well-known for its Romanesque cathedral, provides an amazing look into the history and architecture of the Middle Ages. Wander through the Old Town's winding alleyways, adorned with half-timbered homes and quaint squares, and admire the magnificence of the Speyer Cathedral, a UNESCO World Heritage site.

The Technik Museum Speyer is a must-visit if you want to marvel at antique vehicles like cars, planes, and even a space shuttle.

10. Neckar Valley: Enter the picturesque Neckar Valley by traveling along the Neckar River's meandering course. Discover quaint communities with their own distinct personalities and historic landmarks, such as Neckargemünd and Neckarsteinach. Enjoy leisurely strolls along the riverbanks, stunning vistas from the many lookout spots, and regional food at neighborhood eateries. A tranquil and idyllic retreat from the busy city is available in the Neckar Valley.

11. Heiligenberg: A haven for nature lovers, Heiligenberg is situated close across the Neckar River from Heidelberg. Discover ancient Celtic ruins like the Thingstätte (an outdoor amphitheater) and the Heidenloch (a mystery hole in the ground) by taking a hike through the hill's forested slopes. The Philosopher's Walk is a beautiful trail that winds along the Heiligenberg's slopes, providing sweeping views of Heidelberg.

12. Black Forest: Located a few hours' drive from Heidelberg, the Black Forest will amaze you with its magical splendor. The extensive forested area is well-known for its tall trees, charming towns, and cuckoo clocks. Embark on nature walks to breathtaking waterfalls, take scenic drives along winding roads, and sample traditional Black Forest cuisine. The renowned Black Forest cake, a delightful treat composed with cherries, cream, and chocolate, should not be missed.

13. Hockenheimring: One of Germany's most recognizable racetracks, the Hockenheimring, should be visited by motorsport enthusiasts. To discover the track's past, view the pit lane, and see the facilities, attend a race or take a guided tour. If you're fortunate, you might even have the opportunity to test-drive a fast car.

14. Frankfurt: If you want a really global experience, think about taking a day trip to Frankfurt. This thriving metropolis is renowned for its cutting-edge skyline, elegant old town, and varied cultural landscape.

Explore world-class museums, take a stroll along the Main River promenade, and pay a visit to the Römer, the city's famous medieval town hall. Frankfurt also has a variety of delicious restaurants and fantastic shopping options.

You can discover the region's richness and beauty by traveling past Heidelberg. These adjacent towns and villages provide a richness of adventure and discovery, whether you're fascinated by historic architecture, charmed by cobblestone alleyways, or inspired by the beautiful vistas.

Start an exciting journey as you explore the undiscovered wonders just outside of Heidelberg.

7.2 Schwetzingen Palace: A Secluded Refuge for Lovers

The majestic Schwetzingen Palace is located in the quaint hamlet of Schwetzingen, not far from Heidelberg. Visitors can get a taste of the luxury and grandeur of the Baroque era by visiting this charming palace and its perfectly planted gardens.

Schwetzingen Palace, dubbed "Versailles of the Palatinate," is a real gem that enchants with its architectural magnificence and serene environs. Here is a thorough and in-depth guide to Schwetzingen Palace.

1. History and Architecture: The 14th-century construction of Schwetzingen Palace began as a moated medieval castle. Prince Elector Carl Theodor later rebuilt it into a lavish Baroque palace in the 18th century. The palace displays a tasteful fusion of Baroque, Rococo, and Classical features in its architecture. While the interior enchants guests with richly adorned chambers, opulent furnishings, and magnificent artwork, the exterior of the building exhibits complex ornamentation, stunning facades, and elegant symmetry.

2. The large and well planned gardens at Schwetzingen Palace are the building's real feature. The gardens, which cover over 72 hectares, are a genuine work of landscape architecture. Each part, which is divided into several groups, offers a different mood and aesthetic delight. Discover the beautiful patterns, expertly manicured hedges, and elaborate fountains of the traditional French Garden. Admire the English Garden's magnificence, with its winding walkways, tranquil lakes, and charming bridges. The grounds also have a mosque, an Apollo temple, and an amphitheater, all of which add to the charm and quirkiness of the area.

3. Temple of Mercury: The Temple of Mercury is one of the royal grounds' most recognizable buildings. A real architectural wonder, this circular temple is located on an island in the middle of a serene pond.

The temple is a well-liked venue for peaceful reflection because of its magnificent design and tranquil setting.

4. The Orangery: The spectacular Orangery, a sizable structure with a central hall and arcades, is located next to the palace. The Orangery today serves as a location for performances, exhibitions, and cultural events after originally being used to house delicate citrus trees during the colder months. The Orangery's elegant interior, which features paintings and elaborate embellishments, adds to its grandeur and attractiveness.

5. Cultural Events: The Schwetzingen Palace is a center for culture in addition to being a visual treat. The Schwetzingen Festival, a well-known music festival that draws performers from around the world, is held annually in the palace. Immerse yourself in the world of opera and classical music by attending a concert in the magnificent Orangery or the palace's grounds.

6. Palace Museum: Located inside the palace, the Palace Museum provides information about the past and way of life of the royal inhabitants. Explore the rooms' fine vintage furnishings, dexterous tapestries, and art collections. Discover the histories of the princes and princesses who lived in Schwetzingen Palace in the past.

7. Park Strolls and Picnics: Schwetzingen Palace provides plenty of opportunity for leisurely strolls and picnics in addition to its formal gardens and architectural marvels. Walk down the tree-lined streets, find a quiet area near the lakes, or spread a blanket out on the verdant lawns. It's the ideal place to decompress, unwind, and take in the beauty of nature because of the lovely surroundings.

A trip to Schwetzingen Palace is like entering a storybook. A very magical experience is created by its magnificent architectural design, finely planted grounds, and peaceful atmosphere.

Schwetzingen Palace guarantees to leave a lasting impression and transport you to a bygone era of elegance and grandeur, regardless of your interests in history, art, music, or simply seeking a romantic escape.

7.3 A Journey of Enological Delights: Wine Tasting in the Neckar Valley Vineyards

The Neckar Valley is a region known for its wine making heritage. It has beautiful vistas and moderate slopes. Wine lovers' palates will be delighted by the range of premium wines produced by the vineyards that dot the valley.

Going on a wine tasting tour in the Neckar Valley is a chance to experience the local flavors, learn about winemaking processes, and become immersed in the area's rich viticultural legacy. Here is a thorough and in-depth guide to wine tasting in the vineyards of the Neckar Valley.

1. Vineyard Tours: A guided vineyard tour is a great way to begin your wine-tasting trip. Numerous wineries in the Neckar Valley have tours that take you through the vineyards and give you an understanding of how wine is made from the grape to the glass. Discover the distinctive terroir that shapes the characteristics of the wines as you stroll through the vines and learn about the various grape varieties planted there. Experienced tour guides will impart their knowledge by describing the subtleties of winemaking and the unique qualities of the regional varietals.

2. Experiences with Wine Tasting: After seeing the vineyards, you should enjoy the joy of wine tasting. The Neckar Valley's wineries provide a variety of wine sampling opportunities to suit diverse tastes. There is something for everyone, from relaxed sampling at the cellar door to sommelier-led tours. Learn about the various flavors and smells that characterize each wine varietal as you taste a variety of wines, from delicate reds to crisp whites.

As they can offer insightful information about the wines you're tasting, pay attention to the winemaker's notes and suggestions.

3. Food and Wine Pairing: Attending classes on food and wine pairing will improve your wine tasting experience. Many wineries provide guided tastings where their wines are expertly complemented with regional delicacies. This enables you to investigate how different tastes, textures, and scents interact to create a pleasing blend that improves the enjoyment of both food and wine. Find the ideal pairing for a delicate Riesling and a platter of cheeses made in your area, or for a hearty regional cuisine and a strong red blend.

4. Wine Festivals and Events: The Neckar Valley has a thriving wine culture, and throughout the year, there are numerous wine festivals and events to honor the area's vinicultural heritage. To enjoy the lively environment, sample a wide variety of wines from various producers, and interact with the neighborhood's winemaking community, schedule your visit to coincide with these events. These occasions offer a lively and immersive wine tasting experience, ranging from customary harvest celebrations to wine and culinary fairs.

5. Wine Education: Deepen your understanding of wine by taking part in wine education courses provided by local wine groups or vineyards. Workshops on winemaking techniques, vineyard management, or tasting techniques may be included in these programs. Get to know industry professionals, discover the elements that affect wine quality, and get a greater respect for the skill that went into each bottle.

6. Purchases of Wine: As you tour the vineyards and sample the wines, you'll probably discover a few you'd like to take home. The majority of wineries let customers buy bottles right at the cellar entrance. Profit from this opportunity to stock up on your favored choices so that you can continue to enjoy the wines of the Neckar Valley long after your stay. Additionally, some wineries provide wine clubs or membership services that let you keep up with the region's vinicultural offers while getting regular shipments of their wines.

7. Responsible Wine Tourism: It's important to follow responsible wine tourism principles when partaking in wine tasting events. Pace yourself throughout tastings so you may properly appreciate and assess each wine. To ensure a safe trip if you're driving, think about hiring a local driver or taking public transportation. Respect the grounds of the wineries and the vineyards by adhering to any instructions they may have offered. Finally, keep in mind to drink sensibly and enjoy yourself without going overboard.

A sensory adventure that lets you experience the rich wine tradition of the Neckar Valley is wine tasting. The Neckar Valley offers a comprehensive wine tourism experience, including vineyard exploration, guided tastings, wine and culinary pairings, and immersion in wine-related activities.
Explore the world of enological delights as you learn about the distinctive terroir and flavors of the region's wines.

8. SHOPPING AND ENTERTAINMENT

Heidelberg is a bustling center for shopping and entertainment in addition to being a city of historical and cultural value. Heidelberg has something for everyone, from little boutique stores to busy marketplaces and a wide range of entertainment alternatives.

Use this full and thorough guide to immerse yourself in the city's shopping scene and discover the exciting entertainment locations.

- **Shopping Districts:** Heidelberg has a variety of shopping areas to suit a variety of tastes. A shopper's delight, the Hauptstrasse is one of Europe's longest pedestrian streets. Along its length are a variety of specialty shops selling one-of-a-kind goods, chic booksellers, stylish fashion boutiques, and worldwide brands. Explore the Altstadt (Old Town)'s narrow lanes to find hidden treasures, antique stores, and local artists presenting their work. On the other side of the Neckar River in the Neuenheim neighborhood, you'll find premium boutiques, designer shops, and chic home furnishing businesses.

- **Visit the thriving markets and flea markets** in Heidelberg for a distinctive shopping experience. A regular farmers' market is held on the Marktplatz, where you may buy handcrafted goods, fresh fruit, local cheeses, and baked delicacies. Discover the vibrant atmosphere, interact with the welcoming sellers, and experience the local cuisine. Moreover, keep an eye out for flea markets and vintage markets that occasionally appear and provide a wealth of antiques, collectibles, and one-of-a-kind items.

- Heidelberg is a city that values **art and craftsmanship.** It has galleries and artisan shops. Explore the many galleries and artisan shops dotted across the city to find local artists and craftspeople.

View exhibitions of modern sculptures, paintings, and photographs. Visit ateliers, jewelry stores, and ceramic studios to see how skilled artisans produce one-of-a-kind items. Participate in the work of the artists, discover their methods, and possibly locate a one-of-a-kind artwork to take home as a reminder of your stay in Heidelberg.

- **Entertainment Venues:** Heidelberg has a wide selection of entertainment venues to suit a variety of tastes. One of Germany's oldest theaters, the Heidelberg Theatre, presents a range of productions, such as plays, musicals, and ballets. Spend the evening immersed in the performing arts and taking in some culture. The Philharmonic Orchestra of Heidelberg, known for its superb musicianship, dazzles audiences with its classical performances. Check out the event calendars and enjoy a night of symphonic treats.

- **Music and Nightlife:** After dark, Heidelberg's thriving nightlife culture guarantees that there will never be a dull moment. Visit inviting jazz clubs, bustling pubs, and chic cocktail bars to relax and take in live music performances. The city's rich music scene offers everything from rock and electronic music to jazz and blues. Come experience the vibrant atmosphere with locals and other tourists while dancing the night away.

- **Street Performances & Festivals:** Throughout the year, Heidelberg comes to life with festivals and street performances that highlight the artistic flair of the city. A lively atmosphere is created by the street musicians, artists, and entertainers who enthrall onlookers with their skills. A great way to experience the local culture and take in interesting performances is to keep an eye out for festivals honoring music, art, film, and literature.

- Enjoy **Heidelberg's delectable cuisine** while shopping or taking in one of the city's many entertainment alternatives. There are many cafes, restaurants, and diners in the city where you may enjoy both local specialties and delicacies from around the world. Enjoy a leisurely meal at a welcoming bistro and sample regional favorites such as schnitzel or sauerkraut, and indulge in delectable pastries and desserts in delightful bakeries.

- **Cultural Encounters:** The city of Heidelberg is proud of its cultural heritage. Utilize the countless museums, art galleries, and cultural institutions that provide enlightening experiences. Discover the history of the area while admiring the Kurpfälzisches Museum's extensive collection of artwork and artifacts. Explore the Heidelberg University Museum to see examples of the university's historical contributions to science and culture.

To learn more about the city's cultural heritage, take part in workshops, lectures, or tours led by cultural experts.

- **Wellness and Rest:** Reward yourself with some well-earned rest after a day of shopping and amusement. There are many spas and health facilities in Heidelberg where you may revitalize your body and mind. Enjoy opulent spa services, relax in saunas and steam rooms, or have a relaxing massage. To unwind in the fresh air, take a leisurely stroll along the Neckar River's banks or locate a quiet area in one of the city's parks.

Heidelberg combines shopping with entertainment, providing a wide range of delights and experiences. Explore the city's many shopping areas, visit local markets and artisan stores, take in musical and theatrical acts, and sample the cuisine.

Heidelberg provides everything you're looking for, whether you're looking for unusual treasures, cultural activities, or an exciting nightlife, making sure your trip is full of special moments and pleasurable discoveries.

8.1 Finding Pleasures in Boutiques and Specialty Shops

Heidelberg offers a large selection of boutiques and specialized shops that appeal to a variety of tastes and interests, making it a refuge for those who enjoy retail therapy.

The city's shopping environment is likely to be exciting, with everything from trendy boutiques to distinctive stores selling locally produced goods. With the help of this thorough and in-depth guide, indulge in some much-needed retail therapy.

1. One of Europe's longest pedestrian thoroughfares, **Hauptstrasse**, is a great place to start your shopping expedition. This busy avenue is lined with a diverse assortment of stores, from national chains to neighborhood businesses. Discover the trendy shops that feature

the newest styles in apparel, accessories, and footwear. Find distinctive jewelry, chic home accents, and high-quality leather products. Take your time looking around the shops since you never know what treasures you might find.

2.   Step into Heidelberg's Altstadt to experience its alluring charm and discover a wealth of speciality shops and boutiques. Discover charming stores selling artisanal goods, handmade crafts, and vintage mementos as you stroll through the cobblestone streets. Visit art galleries exhibiting regional talent, bookstores with a large selection of books on literature and the arts, and antique stores brimming with vintage finds. The Altstadt is the ideal location to find special mementos to bring home.

3. Cross the charming Old Bridge to reach **Neuenheim**, a district renowned for its premium boutiques and specialized shops. Designer clothing, high-end leather products, and opulent home

furnishings are all available here. Explore the world of fashion and elegance by perusing the exquisite boutiques. Additionally, Neuenheim has a wide variety of gourmet food stores where you may satiate your cravings for regional specialties, premium wines, and handcrafted chocolates.

4. **Markets:** Take in the lively atmosphere of Heidelberg's markets, where you can buy a wide variety of regional goods and fresh fruit. You may immerse yourself in the hues and flavors of the area at the regular farmers' market that takes place on the Marktplatz. Examine fresh produce such as fruits, vegetables, cheeses, and baked items. Speak with amiable merchants who take pride in their wares. Watch out for seasonal markets and craft festivals where regional artisans sell their handmade goods.

5. **Heidelberg University:** Take some time to browse the shops and stores in the area. This area offers a distinctive shopping experience, with everything from hip designer boutiques to student-run shops. Find unique accessories, vintage apparel, and independent designers that capture the lively and youthful energy of the campus community. It's a great place to find fashionable and unique products that make you stand out from the crowd.

6. Heidelberg is home to a wide variety of specialist shops that appeal to particular passions and interests. You can locate specialty stores that satisfy your needs, whether you're a tea connoisseur, a bookworm, or an expert on exquisite wines. Discover tea stores that offer a wide range of unusual mixes and accessories. Explore bookstores offering a diverse selection of books in a range of genres and language.

7. **Local Goods and Crafts:** Discover shops that feature goods and crafts manufactured locally to fully immerse yourself in Heidelberg's culture. These shops provide a window into the artistic past of the city, selling everything from handcrafted jewelry and pottery to traditional apparel and specialty food items. Support regional makers and bring home one-of-a-kind mementos that capture Heidelberg's genuine spirit.

8. Cafes and delis: Grab a snack as you indulge in retail therapy. Visit one of Heidelberg's beautiful cafes or delis for a break. Savor delicious pastries and sandwiches while sipping coffee or tea. Many stores have inviting cafes on the premises, providing a calm and comfortable atmosphere to unwind and recharge.

In Heidelberg, retail therapy is more than simply window shopping; it's also about getting to know the city's distinct personality and soaking up its energetic atmosphere.

Discover items that capture the spirit of Heidelberg by perusing the boutiques and specialty shops, interacting with regional craftspeople, and shopping there.

The city's retail scene provides a unique shopping experience full of wonderful surprises, whether you're looking for fashion, regional goods, or handmade crafts.

Heidelberg's Exciting Nightlife: A Guide to the City's Bars, Clubs, and Live Music Venues

Heidelberg is a dynamic destination for nightlife lovers in addition to being a city of historical and cultural attractions. As the sun sets, a wide variety of bars, clubs, and live music venues open up around the city, catering to a wide range of interests and preferences. Utilize this in-depth guide to Heidelberg's nightlife to experience the vibrant and vivacious atmosphere.

1. Hauptstrasse: In addition to being a bustling shopping district, Hauptstrasse is also a center for the city's nightlife. A variety of taverns and pubs with various ambiances and vibes can be found here. There is something for everyone, whether you want to spend a peaceful evening with friends or a fun-filled party atmosphere. As you take in the colorful energy of the city, enjoy craft beers, specialty cocktails, and a large selection of spirits.

2. Untere Strasse: is a bustling street dotted with taverns and pubs that draws both locals and tourists. It is tucked away in Heidelberg's Old Town. Investigate the quaint and private places where you may spend a laid-back evening with beverages and discussions. As you immerse yourself in the genuine Heidelberg nightlife, feel the wonderful welcome of the inhabitants.

3. Studentenkneipen: Heidelberg is home to one of Germany's oldest and most prominent universities, and the city's thriving nightlife is a result of the student population. Learn about the student pubs, or studentenkneipen, which provide a distinctive and lively ambiance. These places provide inexpensive beverages, live music, and the ability to mix with the neighborhood's young professionals and students.

4. Clubs & Dance Floors: Heidelberg boasts a number of clubs and dance floors to satisfy your demands for a night of dancing and pounding beats. The city offers a wide variety of possibilities, from mainstream clubs playing the newest songs to underground places hosting electronic music events. Don your dancing shoes and have fun on the dance floor while DJs play music that will keep the party going all night long.

5. Live Music Venues: Heidelberg boasts a flourishing live music scene that features both local musicians and acts from around the world. Investigate locations where live performances take place, from secluded acoustic gigs to exhilarating concerts. There is a genre to fit every preference, ranging from rock and indie to jazz and blues.

Experience the thrilling energy of a live performance as you lose yourself in the alluring sounds of brilliant musicians.

6. Wine Bars and Tasting Rooms: Heidelberg, a city located in the famous German wine region, is the ideal location to have a classy and refined evening. Learn about wine appreciation at wine bars and tasting facilities where you may savor delectable regional wines. Enjoy the laid-back atmosphere, competent sommeliers, and carefully chosen wines that highlight the area's rich viticultural legacy.

7. Heidelberg also hosts a number of **cultural events and festivals** that provide interesting nocturnal experiences. There is always something going on in the city, from outdoor concerts and theater performances to art exhibits and movie showings. Look out upcoming events in the area, get involved in the rich cultural activities, and get into the Heidelberg mood.

8. After a night of celebration, visit one of Heidelberg's **late-night restaurants** to sate your appetite. You can choose from a range of meals to satisfy your hunger, whether you're craving a meaty kebab, a juicy burger, or a tasty slice of pizza. These places are designed with night owls in mind, so you can refuel and recharge before returning to the city.

After the sun sets, Heidelberg's nightlife scene provides a dynamic and varied choice of events that will help you make priceless memories.

The city has something to suit every mood and taste, whether you want a warm pub, an exciting club, or a small live music venue.
Immerse yourself in Heidelberg's exciting nightlife and let the city's energy seduce you.

8.3   Special Gifts and Souvenirs to Bring Home

When you go to Heidelberg, you'll want to bring a little bit of its allure and personality back with you. Thankfully, the city has a plenty of one-of-a-kind gifts and souvenirs that showcase its rich history, cultural heritage, and regional craftsmanship.

Here is a full and comprehensive list of the special gifts and mementos you may take home from Heidelberg, ranging from vintage relics to modern innovations.

1. Memorabilia: from the famous Heidelberg Castle is available for purchase. These items include postcards, magnets, and keychains that feature gorgeous pictures of the castle. The castle's reproduction models and tiny figures that perfectly depict its architectural grandeur are also available. The most recognizable landmark in the city and its historical significance are commemorated by these artifacts.

2. Student Memorabilia and Caps: Heidelberg is known for its prestigious university, and you can enjoy the student lifestyle by purchasing a traditional student cap, also known as a "Mütze." These caps, decorated with vibrant ribbons, are a representation of the city's academic traditions. To honor your connection to Heidelberg's intellectual spirit, you can also find additional university-themed mementos including t-shirts, hoodies, and stationary.

3. Beer Steins & Glassware: Heidelberg shares the nation of Germany's famed beer culture. Bring a typical beer stein or a set of beer glasses with the name or symbol of the city with you. These genuine glassware items are not only useful but also make very interesting and beautiful gifts. In addition to serving as a reminder of the pleasurable times spent in Heidelberg's beer gardens and pubs, they let you bring a taste of German beer culture into your own house.

4. German crafts: Browse the stores in Heidelberg's Old Town to get top-notch souvenirs made of traditional German crafts. Look for exquisite Christmas ornaments, elaborate cuckoo clocks, or hand-carved wooden figurines. These products are emblematic of Germany's rich artistic past and make thoughtful presents that highlight the nation's attention to detail and craftsmanship.

5. Local Cuisine and Beverage Specialties: Heidelberg and the area around it are renowned for their delectable cuisine. Think about taking back locally produced treats like delectable chocolates, gourmet mustard, artisanal cheeses, or a bottle of wine. These tasty keepsakes are a delicious way to remember Heidelberg long after your trip and make thoughtful presents that may be given to loved ones.

6. Handmade Jewelry and Accessories: Heidelberg is home to outstanding craftspeople who produce one-of-a-kind jewelry and accessories. Look for handcrafted jewelry such as bracelets, rings, earrings, and necklaces that include pearls, gemstones, or delicate metalwork.

These one-of-a-kind things offer a distinctive and fashionable souvenir of your time in Heidelberg while also reflecting the artistic essence of the city.

7. Books & Literature: Heidelberg has a long literary tradition that you can discover by buying books and works of literature about the area. Look for writings by well-known writers who were influenced by Heidelberg, such as Mark Twain or Johann Wolfgang von Goethe. Along with local poetry, history books, and travel guides that explore the city's unique past, you may find their writings online. These literary mementos offer a greater appreciation of Heidelberg's cultural importance and make lovely presents for bookworms.

8. Local Artwork and Prints: Heidelberg has a thriving art community, and you may show your support by buying local artists' paintings or prints. Find paintings, photos, or prints that beautifully depict Heidelberg's landscapes, landmarks, or street scenes by browsing art galleries and studios.

These items enable you to serve as a permanent memory of the aesthetic charm of the city and to bring a touch of Heidelberg's artistic expression into your house.

Prioritize quality, authenticity, and a personal connection to the history and culture of the city when selecting Heidelberg-made gifts and souvenirs. These one-of-a-kind products, which can range in size from a tiny trinket to a big work of art, can act as physical mementos of your time in Heidelberg and bring back pleasant memories for years to come.

9. USEFUL TRAVEL ADVICE

Making travel plans to Heidelberg? With these thorough and in-depth practical travel recommendations, you can guarantee a smooth and joyful vacation.

These suggestions will enable you to get the most out of your trip to this stunning city, from pre-trip planning to on-the-ground assistance.

1. Documents for Travel and Insurance:
- Verify that your passport is valid for at least six months after the date you want to depart.
- Prior to entering Germany, make sure you have all relevant visas.
- Take into account getting travel insurance to safeguard oneself from unforeseeable events like trip cancellations, medical emergencies, or lost luggage.

2. Ideal Season to Visit:
- Although Heidelberg has a moderate climate, the seasons might change. When the weather is beautiful and the city is bustling, the spring (April to June) and fall (September to October) are the busiest travel seasons.

- Hotel rates may increase throughout the summer (July to August) due to the increased number of travelers. There are less people around yet it's colder in winter (December to February).
- Review the calendar of local events and festivals to schedule your trip around any interesting cultural festivals.

3. How to travel to Heidelberg:

- Frankfurt Airport (FRA), which is about 90 kilometers distant, is the closest sizable airport. Heidelberg is easily accessible by train, bus, or vehicle from the airport.
- If traveling by train, the Heidelberg Hauptbahnhof is a convenient location with frequent direct connections to major German cities and nearby nations.

4. How to Get Around Heidelberg:

- The best way to see Heidelberg's city core is on foot. Being a pedestrian-friendly area, the Altstadt (Old Town) allows you to stroll through its picturesque streets and explore important attractions.

- Buses and trams are two modes of public transit that offer easy links to the city's various locations.
- Take into account getting a HeidelbergCARD, which grants access to unrestricted citywide public transit as well as savings on attractions.

5. Accommodation:
- Heidelberg has a selection of lodging choices, including hotels, inns, and apartments. Prioritize your hotel reservations, especially during the busiest travel times.
- If you want to be close to the main attractions and the bustling city center, think about lodging in the Altstadt. Another well-liked neighborhood with a pleasant vibe is Neuenheim, which is across the Neckar River.

6. Payment and Currency:
- The Euro (EUR) is the unit of currency in Germany. It is advisable to have some cash on hand for modest expenditures and emergency situations.
- Although most businesses take credit cards, it is always a good idea to have some cash on hand.

- If you need to withdraw money from an ATM, there are plenty of them in the city.

7. Language:
- German is the official language of Germany. Even if the majority of Heidelberg residents can communicate in English to some degree, knowing a few fundamental German words will improve your trip and demonstrate respect for the community.

8. Safety:
Heidelberg is a fairly safe city, but it's always crucial to be on guard and adopt the appropriate security measures.
- Keep an eye on your belongings and be mindful of your surroundings, especially in crowded places.
- Store a duplicate of crucial papers, such as your passport and travel insurance, in a safe place apart from the originals.

9. Local customs and etiquette:
- Since Germans place a high importance on timeliness, it is customary to keep scheduled appointments and reservations.

- It is traditional to wait for everyone's food to arrive before beginning the meal when dining out. Don't forget to tip roughly 10% of the whole amount.
- Pay attention to noise levels, particularly in populated places and during calm hours.

You'll be well-equipped to explore Heidelberg and make priceless vacation memories if you heed these helpful travel advice. Take in the beauty and culture of the city, and feel the friendliness of the locals.

9.1 Options for Getting Around Heidelberg by Transportation

Heidelberg provides a variety of transportation choices to make it simple for you to get around the city and its surroundings. Here is a thorough and exhaustive guide to traveling around Heidelberg, whether you like to explore on foot, take public transportation, or rent a car.

1. Walking:
- The best way to see Heidelberg's city core, notably the Altstadt (Old Town), is on foot. It is simple to roam the city and take in its attractiveness due to its small size and pedestrian-friendly streets.
- The majority of the top sights, such Heidelberg Castle and the Church of the Holy Spirit, are strollable from one another. Enjoy the architecture, the lively ambiance, and the leisurely stroll through the cobblestone streets.

2. Using Public Transit:
- *Buses:* The Rhein-Neckar-Verkehr (RNV) runs an effective bus system in Heidelberg. Buses travel throughout the entire city, making it simple to get to various areas and tourist destinations.

- *Trams:* There is a tram system in the city that offers additional transit choices. In order to get to places outside of the city center, including Neuenheim or the Heidelberg Central Station, trams are especially helpful.

- *Tickets:* You can buy tickets from the bus or tram driver directly, via ticket vending machines, or via a mobile ticketing app.

If you want to use public transit regularly, think about purchasing a day pass or multi-day pass.

3. Bicycles:

Heidelberg is a bike-friendly city, so taking a bike for a spin is a great way to see the city at your own leisure. Bicycles can be rented at various rental businesses for an hourly, daily, or weekly fee.

-Bicycles are safe and fun throughout the city thanks to the designated bike lanes and well-maintained bicycle infrastructure. You can tour the city's scenic places with the use of maps and suggested routes that some rental shops offer.

4. Ridesharing and Taxis:

- Taxis are easy to find in Heidelberg, and you can easily hire one using a taxi app or at designated taxi stops. Taxis are a practical choice when you need to cover greater distances or have big luggage.

- Ridesharing services like Uber are also accessible in Heidelberg, providing a practical and frequently more cost-effective substitute for standard taxis.

5. Renting a car:

- Renting a car is an alternative to think about if you want the independence of owning your own vehicle. You can reserve a car for the duration of your stay at one of the many car rental companies in Heidelberg.

- It's crucial to keep in mind that parking in the city center might be difficult and pricey. If parking is an issue, think about asking your lodging about it or using one of the many public parking garages outside the city center.

6. Ferries on the Neckar River:

- Take a Neckar River ferry for an interesting mode of transportation and to take in the surrounding scenery. The Neckar River is the route of these boats, which connect a number of locations, including Heidelberg and nearby towns like Neckarsteinach.

- Neckar River boats provide a relaxing opportunity to see the area and its beautiful scenery. Depending on your inclination, you can choose between brief visits and full-day excursions.

Depending on your timetable and interests, take into account a combination of walking, public transit, and other modes when you plan your transportation in Heidelberg.

Take advantage of these alternatives' comfort and adaptability to make the most of your time in this fascinating city.

9.2 Tips on Choosing Accommodations to Ensure a Memorable Stay

The ideal lodging must be selected if you want to have a wonderful stay in Heidelberg. The city has a variety of options to accommodate all tastes and price ranges. To assist you in selecting the ideal lodging, the following extensive and comprehensive recommendations are provided:

1. Hotels:
- Heidelberg has a wide selection of hotels, from opulent five-star inns to reasonably priced lodgings. Major attractions are easily accessible due to the abundance of hotels that are

conveniently situated in or close to the city center.

- For a truly stunning vacation, search for hotels with views of the Neckar River or the old cityscape. Additionally, some hotels provide extras like spa services, rooftop lounges, and on-site dining options.

- Popular neighborhoods with easy access to attractions, a variety of restaurants, and a lively environment include the Altstadt (Old Town) and Neuenheim.

2. Bed and breakfasts and guesthouses:

- Think about booking a room in a guesthouse or bed and breakfast for a more individualized and private experience. With hosts who may provide local knowledge and recommendations, these accommodations frequently offer a pleasant and homey ambiance.

- There are guesthouses and B&Bs all across the city, particularly in quaint residential areas. Typically, they provide cozy lodging, a sumptuous breakfast, and friendly service.

3. Vacation Rentals and Apartments:

- Renting an apartment or holiday home in Heidelberg is a great option if you value flexibility and privacy. For individuals who are traveling with families or larger groups, or for extended vacations, this choice is especially practical.

Apartments and vacation homes offer a "home away from home" feeling thanks to features like fully furnished kitchens, living rooms, and occasionally outdoor spaces. Both the city's center and the nearby areas contain them.

4. Castle Inns:

Consider staying at one of the castle hotels nearby Heidelberg for a genuinely distinctive and memorable experience. These old castles and palaces have been transformed into opulent lodgings that combine history and comfort.

- Castle hotels frequently provide breathtaking views, opulent accommodations, and first-rate services. They provide you the chance to become fully immersed in the area's rich history and have a genuinely regal experience.

5. Alternative Facilities:

- Alternative lodging alternatives in Heidelberg include hostels, boutique hotels, and eco-friendly lodges. These choices offer unique experiences and appeal to various preferences.
- Hostels offer inexpensive lodging and chances to meet other travelers. Boutique hotels offer distinctive interior design and attentive service. Eco-friendly hotels put an emphasis on environmental initiatives and sustainability.

Consider things like location, amenities, budget, and the experience you want when choosing your lodging. It is advised to make reservations in advance, especially during the busiest travel times, to ensure your preferred choice.

Heidelberg offers a wide variety of lodging options, so you can be sure to find a cozy and pleasant place to stay. This will allow you to fully experience the city's joys and make lifelong memories.

9.3 Important German Words and Cultural Customs

In order to improve your experience and respect local traditions, it is good to grasp some fundamental German words and cultural etiquette before visiting Heidelberg. An in-depth and thorough overview to key German expressions and social customs is provided below:

1. Greetings and Foundational Words:
 - Guten Tag: Good day
  - Hallo: Hello
  - Bitte: Please
  - Danke: Thank you
  - Entschuldigung: Excuse me
  - Sprechen Sie Englisch?: Do you speak English?
  - Ja: Yes
  - Nein: No
  - Wie geht es Ihnen?: How are you?
  - Ich verstehe nicht: I don't understand

2. Etiquette and Politeness:
- Germans prioritize timeliness and are kind. Respect is shown by showing up on time for appointments and reservations.

- When greeting someone, give them a strong handshake, make eye contact, and use their title and last name until you're specifically asked to use their first name.
- It's customary to greet employees with **"Guten Tag" or "Hallo"** while entering businesses, eateries, or public areas.
- When making requests or asking for help, always say **"Bitte" (please).**
- Tipping is expected at restaurants and while receiving services. Unless a service charge is already included, it is customary to leave a tip of 10% to 15%.
- It's usual to provide a small present for the host while visiting someone at home, such as flowers or a bottle of wine.

3. Getting Snacks and Drinks:
Please provide a menu, in German:
- Eine Speisekarte, bitte: A menu, please.
- Ich hätte gerne...: I would like...
- Die Rechnung, bitte: The bill, please.
- Prost: Cheers
- Guten Appetit: Enjoy your meal

4. Requesting Directions:
- Entschuldigung, können Sie mir helfen?: Excuse me, can you help me?
- Wo ist...?: Where is...?
- Geradeaus: Straight ahead
- Links: Left
- Rechts: Right

5. Emergency Terminology:
- Hilfe!: Help!
- Ich brauche einen Arzt: I need a doctor.
- Wo ist die nächste Apotheke?: Where's the nearest pharmacy?

When speaking German, keep in mind to talk slowly and clearly so that the natives will understand you and be more inclined to help you.

Despite the fact that many Germans can speak English, it is polite to try utilizing some basic German before switching to English.

It will improve your trip experience and demonstrate your appreciation for the local culture if you take the effort to learn and utilize a few basic German words and become familiar with cultural customs. Enjoy your stay in Heidelberg and seize the chance to interact with the locals.

9.4 Vital Information and Emergency Numbers

To protect your safety and well-being while visiting Heidelberg, it is crucial to have access to crucial contacts and emergency numbers. Here is a thorough list of crucial contacts and emergency numbers you should keep on hand:

1. Emergency Services:
    - Emergency Services: Dial 112 for all emergencies, including police, fire, and medical emergencies. This number can be dialed free of charge from any phone.
    - Police: If you need to report a non-emergency crime or seek assistance from the police, dial 110.

2. Medical Assistance:

- Medical Emergency: In case of a medical emergency, dial **112** for an ambulance or emergency medical services.

- Hospital: Universitätsklinikum Heidelberg (Heidelberg University Hospital) is a renowned medical institution in Heidelberg. Address: **Im Neuenheimer Feld 400, 69120 Heidelberg**.

3. Tourist Information:

- Heidelberg Visitor Center: The official tourist information center provides helpful information about attractions, events, and city tours. **Address: Neckarmünzgasse 1, 69117 Heidelberg.**

4. Consulates and Embassies:

- If you need assistance from your country's consulate or embassy, here are the contact details for a few of them in Heidelberg:

- United States Consulate: Address: **U.S. Consulate General Frankfurt, Gießener Str. 30, 60435 Frankfurt am Main.**

- United Kingdom Consulate: Address: **British Consulate General Frankfurt,**

Zeppelinallee 35, 60325 Frankfurt am Main.

- Canadian Consulate: Address: **Canadian Consulate General Frankfurt, Zeppelinallee 27, 60325 Frankfurt am Main.**

- Australian Consulate: Address: **Australian Consulate General Frankfurt, Main Tower, 28th floor, Neue Mainzer Str. 52-58, 60311 Frankfurt am Main.**

5. Loss or Theft of Documents:

- If you misplace your passport or any other crucial documents, get in touch with the consulate or embassy of your nation right away for advice on what to do. They will offer guidance and support.

6. Transportation:

- **Heidelberg Hauptbahnhof:** The main train station in Heidelberg. It is located in the city center and provides connections to other cities in Germany and Europe. Address: **Willy-Brandt-Platz 5, 69115 Heidelberg.**

- **Public Transportation Hotline:** For information on local transportation services and schedules, you can contact the **Rhein-Neckar-Verkehr GmbH hotline at +49 621 1077077.**

7. Travel Protection:
- Travel insurance is always advised when visiting Heidelberg or any other location. Make sure you have access to your insurance company's contact information as well as any relevant policy information.

Throughout your visit to Heidelberg, keep these crucial contacts and emergency numbers in a location that is secure and convenient.

You can manage any unforeseen events and make sure you can get aid when you need it by being ready with this knowledge. Have a great time while you're in Heidelberg and a safe journey!

10. CONCLUSION

In conclusion, the city of Heidelberg fascinates tourists with its fascinating past, beautiful architecture, and lively culture. You now have access to a wealth of knowledge to make the most of your trip to Heidelberg thanks to this thorough travel guide.

Heidelberg was introduced to you at the outset, laying the groundwork for your exploration. Along with learning about the city's charm and allure, you also gained useful tourist knowledge regarding things like visa procedures and currency conversion.

Then we went into detail about Heidelberg's highlights, taking you to its famous sites. You discovered the beauty that Heidelberg has to offer, from the imposing Heidelberg Castle, which offers sweeping city views, to the charming streets of the Old Town (Altstadt), with its cobblestone streets and historical sites.

You also learned about the city's landmark Church of the Holy Spirit as well as the off-the-beaten-path treasures. You were able to appreciate Heidelberg's appeal in its lesser-known facets by exploring hidden courtyards, obscure streets, and peaceful gardens.

We visited museums, galleries, and exhibitions highlighting art and history to fully immerse ourselves in the history and culture of the city. Additionally, you learned about the celebrations and cultural activities that liven up the city all year long.

No Heidelberg travel guide would be complete without recommending trying some of the regional cuisine. We relished in traditional German fare and local delicacies to provide you with an exquisite dining experience. You had the chance to explore Heidelberg's flavors through suggestions for authentic dining establishments, beer gardens, and local brews to sample.

Heidelberg, though, is about more than just history and culture. We went on outdoor excursions and discovered the city's parks, gardens, and other scenic areas. There were plenty of outdoor activities to choose from, including bicycling and hiking as well as Neckar River cruises and water sports.

We offered suggestions for visiting neighboring cities and villages for Heidelberg day trips. You had the chance to broaden your horizons by visiting Schwetzingen Palace, a romantic hideaway, or by going wine tasting in the Neckar Valley vineyards.

We also looked into Heidelberg's retail and entertainment possibilities, which ranged from lively nightlife options like bars, clubs, and live music venues to retail therapy in boutiques and specialized shops. You found one-of-a-kind presents and mementos to take back home, leaving lasting impressions of your time in Heidelberg.

We closed with useful travel advice, including key German words and cultural etiquette, directions to Heidelberg, and suggestions for accommodations for a wonderful visit. To protect your safety and well-being throughout your vacation, we also supplied crucial contacts and emergency numbers.

Every traveler can find something to like in Heidelberg, which skillfully combines history, culture, and natural beauty. With this thorough travel manual in your hands, you are equipped to explore Heidelberg's joys, uncover its secrets, and reveal its beauty.

Enjoy your journey and your passport to wonderful experiences in Heidelberg!

Printed in Great Britain
by Amazon

39322368R00086